# Built, Not Born

TRENTON T. BUELL

ONE ENTREPRENEUR'S JOURNEY FROM
*NOTHING TO EVERYTHING*

Printed in the United States of America

First Printing, 2025

ISBN  979-8-89390-057-6

Library of Congress Control Number: Pending

Ordering Information: Special discounts are available on quantity purchases by bookstores, corporations, associations, and others. For details, contact the publisher at sales@braughlerbooks.com or at 937-58-BOOKS.

For questions or comments about this book, please write to info@braughlerbooks.com.

**Braughler Books**

braughlerbooks.com

# Contents

## *Introduction*

By the age of twenty-five, I have lived three different lives, I have lived in multiple different homes, I have endured unparalleled abuse. It was at this moment I chose to never let poverty and statistics define me. My story is not the white picket fence we all read about. These words are my escape from the past that still haunts me. I started writing to get all these troubled thoughts out of my head. Curating this was more of a therapy session than writing a book. Through constant pain and failure. I felt that writing all of this down on pages could really work for me. Getting all of the junk out and moving forward. You will get a firsthand glimpse of how choices throughout your life will define you. As you read though the book you will see the ups and downs that shaped me into the serial entrepreneur I am today. You flip a switch and suddenly you want to create more and more companies. I consider this book to be a success if it helps one person.

You are not a product of your environment;

*you get to choose.*

Defy the odds? Or settle for ordinary.

**The choice is yours.**

*Chapter One*

# Identity

When we are born, do we know who we are? Where we should be? How do we fit into this life? I always knew I was different; from the time I could walk, I always seemed to take the path of the most resistance. Why was this?

Growing up in rural Okeana, Ohio, things were simple; cars were simple, people were predictable, and you could look at most people and line up their entire lives and stories by simple judgment. Most people who lived there grew up and lived their whole lives there. Most people had zero desire to leave. Everyone seemed to fit the mold that their parents had made for them. It's crazy to think that most of the way you behave, and your thoughts, are drilled into your head before you can speak. The way you carry yourself is a portion of someone else's, not your identity; think deeply and hard about why you like the things you do. Did someone tell you to, or did you figure out that portion all on your own?

Most of the families had been molded into the norm. The expectation is simple: the American dream. Go to school, get a good job working for a great company, set up retirement, find a special someone, get married, buy a house, fill it with children, and wait for your life to expire. That is what is taught; it is unbelievable that people still accept this as normal.

What happens if you challenge the norm? What happens if you shake it up? What happens if you smash that normal into a million pieces and toss them from the window? What happens when you start thinking, Is this the life I want to live?

Then there is me. My story is crazy.

Shockingly, I made it through some of the things I had seen and situations I was put into. I was number five of six siblings. I never knew they were not my full siblings. It was not until I was at school that a friend explained the concept of half-siblings. It is such a weird way to label blood family members. I guess in a society of crazy labels, everything must be labeled. I would not say I like labels. I am me. That is it, nothing else.

We all had the same mother, but there were three different fathers. Most of my siblings were star athletes; they were taught to love sports by the toxic masculinity that was all around us. They were to be involved in sports, nothing else. My mother loved sports. She was always active. Considering she had me at thirty-eight and my sister at forty, she would have to be active.

As I am writing this, I am in my mid-thirties. I have no children and can't imagine having an infant at this point in my life.

Throughout my traditional upbringing, I couldn't wrap my head around people just being okay with the mundane life. The poverty I endured didn't seem so bad as a child; my mother was a single mom of four on welfare. I am that story. We did have nicer clothes for the most part; my mom would make us look like a million bucks even if we didn't have two quarters to rub together. Despite my mother's best efforts to stay above the curve of poverty, she gave us the best life she could. It's hard to take your parents off the pedestal but remember they are also just trying to make it through life and raise kiddos that aren't complete assholes.

My bio dad saw a meal ticket and took it. My mother was and still is stunning. He dug his fangs into her so badly she didn't know it was happening till it was done. He decided he didn't want to be a dad; he didn't want to grow up, even though I think at this point he has ten or so children, all of whom he abandoned.

He was married to my mother but had another family on the side. A family where I have other siblings born in between each of my siblings' birthdays. I have never understood that mentality. If you are unhappy, leave. Do not take everyone down with you.

My home was a three-bedroom trailer. We had a good little spot, considering the alternative areas we could have lived in and escaped from. A little farm town and living in a trailer seem quite all right. Our home had no air conditioning, an extreme luxury we couldn't afford. Most breezes came from fans in windows, sometimes making the summer nights bearable. In colder months, the furnace only worked half the time, or we couldn't afford the propane bill. The floors were rigged up with street signs and cinder blocks from beneath to keep us from falling through. Molded and sopping wet particleboard made up the flooring, which had disintegrated years prior. Sometimes, the roof leaked. This normally happened in the winter when snow would sit on the roof and melt. Still, Mom made it home with the very little we had.

She had taken so much emotional and physical abuse from the sperm donor that it was tough for her to see straight. He would pop in occasionally to sleep off his drug bender and stay long enough to make our lives a complete living hell. Then, poof, he was gone again, and we were left to pick up the pieces.

Cats ripped the air vents off the floors, and would run through the trailer randomly throughout the night. Or snakes. An opossum found its way into Mom's bedroom one night. Looking back now, these memories are so foreign and distant memory. Like, damn, was that my life? At times, the water was ice cold; the water heater had been rigged so often throughout the year that it finally blew out. It continued to leak for several years. This is where my mother's health started to take a turn.  The black mold that accumulated from this leak was unbearable. I think it made her question everything.

We were no strangers to the behavioral unit in the hospitals; my mother had multiple nervous breakdowns. Who could blame her? I am unsure I could have made it out of her life with a smile. In some ways, she is the strongest woman I have ever met. It is wild to think of her in that way.  To this day my mother continues to struggle. Life has beat her down. Some days she is just out of it. Most women could not have handled the life she did, and she continues to smile.

My education had been put on the back burner; I barely made it out of school. Walking my mother off a ledge would become the norm starting at age thirteen. She struggles with bipolar depression. She would have extremely high highs and extremely low lows. Most of my life growing up was spent making sure she would be okay.

Just because someone carries it well does not mean it is not heavy. There had to be a catastrophe for things to seem normal in our lives. I did not know any difference. These catastrophes become normal for the next several decades of my life. They would manifest their ugly heads into my adulthood. Can people overcome this sort of upbringing? We had been labeled as "those kids," her kids, the trash kids—the bad influences. What we saw at such a young age is that there is no way we could ever overcome the extreme challenges of poverty, poor education, poor guidance, and mental health issues. What's the old saying? "You are a product of your environment."

I refused to settle for that kind of life or unfair label. It's a label I hated; however, I learned to love it. When you defy the odds, it's a great reminder. It is easy to cast judgment. You know nothing of the situation and get to throw your two cents in and walk away without even a second thought. What is hard is understanding mind processes, empathy, and compassion. In a world where you can be anything, just be KIND. You never know what struggles people are dealing with, and you are arrogant enough to think you are better than anyone else. On multiple occasions, I had to check my arrogance. I do look back.

In most situations, the voice in my head says, "Remember where you come from." I am relatable to most people. I understand empathy and always try to remember everyone has their demons.

# Chapter Two

# Tumultuous Is
# Putting It Lightly

To understand why someone has the drive and ability to overcome and conquer so much. You must pull back the layers. Every layer: the painful ones, the broken ones, the thin ones, and the hidden ones. Where to begin?

A friend who had listened to my stories said, "Wow, you should write a book. She then recommended A Child Called It by Dave Pelzer. You should buy it, like now, if you have not read it. The story is unbearable, but there is beauty on the other side. I read it in a few days because it was so good. My story brought my friend to tears because some elements of that book were similar to my childhood. Life is weird when you see it through the eyes of someone else.

I had my struggles attempting to live with ADHD. I was one of the heavily overmedicated 90's babies. People knew very little about this disorder. They would say, "Just give them Ritalin till they sit still. Oh, a large dose isn't working even though he's 69 pounds in the sixth grade and wearing a size four shoe. Let's throw some Adderall at him. Oh, severe mood swings and suicidal thoughts at ten. Let's push an extended release at him and Ritalin." That made the most sense: "Let's over-medicate him until his identity is no longer in tack."

I became a shell of myself. Then they would say, "He can pay attention now, he's quiet now, he is a zombie. This seems to be working." It was like watching myself from above, almost like an out-of-body experience. I know that seems wild. However, this had become my life.

I had so many thoughts and so many dreams, but the medication kept me from being who I am and what I need. Violent mood swings would follow for a few years. These included any of the following: speaking the most hateful, spiteful, and nasty of things; chasing my siblings with knives or stabbing the doors or sofas; throwing things at my siblings or threatening to kill them.

My older brother jokes about this time in our lives. Although I was much smaller and younger, he feared for his life. He thought I would attempt to kill him in his sleep. I am very loving, and it is hard to picture myself in this state. Phrases would play on repeat when I would be in need or asking for help:

"Did you take your meds today?"

"You're such a baby. Stop crying."

"Get over it."

"You are so sensitive."

The next several years seem to be a blur, as I was in a constant fog of over-medicating. When the meds didn't work, I would be given coffee to sleep—oh, you know, at 9 pm. The amount of torture my body was taking was utterly enormous. The fact that I can put my thoughts to paper today is amazing, considering the conditions I was living in. My mental state was shot from day one. Did anyone ever think, maybe he learns differently? Or maybe he is too young to articulate the words he needs. Maybe he has zero clue what is happening to him.

Emotional breakdowns come from being unable to get the correct words and meanings out. They happen when you are told to internalize emotions and boil them up. "Please don't talk about them. That isn't what we do. Brush them under the rug." I mean, when you start on synthetic meth at six years old, who could? I am not saying those medications can't work. However, the fact they used to medicate children in this manner is frightening. I don't think any kids would have had a chance when they are severely overmedicated.

Being so misunderstood at that age is unbearable; it is hard to put this on paper now. The loneliness that comes with it, I don't think I would wish that on my worst enemy. That is just one small pitfall of the dumpster fire that was my childhood. We can all make our jokes about my parents whooped me with a belt when I was a kid, and I knew how to mind. There is a fine line between discipline and abuse. What about a kid with zero impulse control?

Leather belts would welt my legs and bottom for several years. I would get out of bed, not realizing I was being too loud, and BAM! a harsh whip slapped against my legs and bottom. I wouldn't even see it coming. I did not understand why I was even out of bed. I would be lying if I said that high energy plays a factor. The restlessness never stops. I was given synthetic meth, and people would wonder why I was bouncing off the walls at night.

This is the question: after how many hits and how many welts does it sink in that maybe I had little to no control over myself? I would be fully up and talkative and have zero recollection until the leather belt made its impact. I would carry on full stories in my sleep and not even be aware. BAM, another whack, only this time it was my face.

It was not the leather belt this time. It was the metal belt buckle busting me in the face. Splitting the inside of my lips, I'm not too fond of the taste of blood. It is dreadful. I would then ask myself, what the hell just happened??? I was asleep. Why was he hitting me again? Why is he hitting me in the face?"

Unfortunately, he too had his demons, the man that stepped in to play partial parent so we would have some sort of everyday life. He did the best he could, I suppose. I am unsure what I would do if my wife left me for another man. Then I had to raise the other man's four small children. He took in his ex-wife. He had to step in and help raise these kids he did not ask for in a tiny two-bedroom house. Not to mention, it was eight or so years later. He had raised his kids and now had to raise four other children.

I do believe he tried his best. He wanted to keep us in line. When you have a child with a disorder like this, I am sure it can be challenging. He also had to raise five people on a city salary income.

When the abuse became too much, we would move out of the safety of his walls. It is sad to consider that it was a safer place to live. The next line of abuse would start. I thought all the pain and suffering would be over. It seems this would be the beginning.

There were so many variables that played a part: poor education, severe mental health issues on both sides, drug usage, and alcohol abuse. The normal standard in our lives.

I was in a constant fog of overstimulation and overmedication, where that kind of normalcy didn't seem so bad. Just the four kiddos and momma. It was us against the world, so we thought.

Then the sperm donor was released from jail. Why was he in jail, you ask? He was brought up on charges of selling his prescription Ritalin to an undercover police officer. The sperm donor had AADD, adult attention deficit disorder; it seems he blessed me with that genetic disorder. The only time I can ever remember him being an average parent was when he was released from prison—a concise two-week span of sobriety. Of course, he wanted to pick up where he left off.

He walked out on us with a drug problem when I was four or five, somewhere around that age. He would show up now and again when he wanted to play parent and give my mother pennies to feed her four small children. We should bow down and say that he gave her fifty dollars to feed all of us. What a generous man. He comes and goes, making an excellent salary as a truck driver. Back then, it was about sixty-five thousand dollars a year. It was good money then. I will never understand how someone can walk out on their children and then attempt to come back and play parent; still, to this day, it is mindboggling.

When he was in town, it was dreadful. His drunken stupors and crash sessions in the living room, completely unaware of his surroundings. It did not matter if it was one of his kid's birthdays or if they were hosting a sleepover. He would embarrass or scare the absolute hell out of our friends, who would never be allowed back over. If they were even allowed to talk to us again.

"Those kids are bad news. Stay away from them."

I get it now, and I would not blame them for keeping us from their normal lives. I am sure our home was so severely broken. Most people and friends pitied us. It is awful when you are pitied; the pity invite will never sit well with me. It is unbelievable how your childhood subconsciously carries that word into your thirties. Some of my youngest memories are pretty hurtful ones.

This particular night is still a blur and still stings incredibly deep all these years later. I assume he let my mom down again; she felt she had no one to turn to. Why does he get to walk away from all the responsibilities, and she is forced to care for four children on her own? We were loaded up in the car, late at night. Mom seemed off, unsure what was happening in her mind.

Is she breaking again? I wish I could help her. Why are we heading toward the city?

When we would meet up with the sperm donor, she'd be forced to tolerate him and to do things she didn't want to do. She had to try to keep a roof over our heads. Unfortunately, at whatever means necessary.

I had fallen asleep in the back seat. We awakened, stopped in front of a house. I didn't recognize the house; she said Dad was waiting for us. So we went up to the front door, all four of us. We knocked and knocked, no answer. We turned to head back toward Mom's car to tell her he wasn't answering. At that moment, Mom drove off and left us on the side of the road.

This memory to this day makes me cry. I am currently crying while trying to write this memory. Why would she leave us? Why? Who would leave their kids on the side of the road?

I'm pretty sure this was another mental breakdown for her. She loves her kids more than anything in this world. She must have been pushed so far, but she thought this was the best route she was forced to take.

Eventually, he answered the door. This was his sidepiece's house. He opened the door to find four small children on the lawn with no Mom. He brought us home the next day, and this moment would never be discussed again.

Using her children as tools does nothing but traumatize the kids. The kids always lose in these situations. This is where my abandonment issues come into full swing. I cannot even fathom the amount of pain she was dealing with to be pushed this far. Children used as tools and pawns in their games. My mother has always tried to see the good in people. She has such a kind heart; however, this big heart leaves her open and a target for manipulators. He was a master at manipulation. He could sell sand in the Sahara Desert.

There are some more shattered memories of him coming into town and beating my mom senselessly. Do not get me wrong, she gave him a run for his money, but he always seemed to overpower her kind soul. He was pure evil. He wanted to hurt everyone the way he broke. The way his mother and father hurt him. His mother was another whole level of evil. He had no role model. My father would beat my mother so badly that she wouldn't even speak to us. Some of my earliest memories consist of pain.

One night, after hours of abuse and arguing, he told us to pack our bags. My sister and I, in tears, would get a bag packed. He had us wait by the front door. It was midnight. He said that Children's Services were coming to take us away. He said he did not want to take care of us. "Your Mom cannot either," he told us. He did not want us.

These memories still make me cry to this day. Why did he not want his kids? Were we that bad? Why were we so easily thrown to the side? Discarded like trash.

I was around five to seven years old when this incident occurred. I thank God my sister was too little to remember those horrible times. Who in their right mind tells their kids they do not want them and to pack their belongings? I cannot even bear the thought of saying that to a child? Unfortunately, these are the intricate layers that have to be pulled back.

Another incident I remember was when I was about nine or ten. He had come into town, called me on the phone, and said he was bringing me and sissy Christmas presents. I cautiously kept this information from my sister; I didn't want her to feel the disappointments I had felt consistently.

I am unsure how my intuition kicked in at such a young age. I tried to shield her from the bad, the hurt, and the ugly that was our lives and that man. I kept her from many catastrophic events that made up our lives.

He was late again; it never fails. Sitting, waiting up for him, it was getting late. Mom told us to get in bed because Santa would be here in the morning. Ah, the joys of being a child, when most kids can believe in something other than pain and hurt. It's one of the few things we had to look forward to.

Half the time, starving was better than dealing with him. I would rather have no food if that meant he was out of our lives. However, those times would only last temporarily. He would mentally or physically exhaust my mom to the point she had no energy to fight him to leave.

This is a Christmas Eve I have never been able to block out. He showed up around 1 am. He was a loud son of a bitch; quite literally, if he did not get his way with our mom, he made sure we all suffered. He started yelling; we were all awake now. We lived in a three-bedroom trailer. It isn't like the place was soundproof. He continued to yell and the abuse became so unbearable that survival instincts kicked in. I decided I had enough and yelled, "We are trying to sleep so Santa can come!"

His reply was, "You are so stupid. Santa is not real. Life's a bitch then you die."

I'm pretty sure this is where my innocence was stripped away. I felt myself go numb. Yep, I was stupid to believe in anything other than the harsh reality of my life. He and Mom started going at it again; more screams, more slurs, and profanity followed. She threatened to call the police, then yelled, "Merry Fucking Christmas!" he then proceeded to slam the door several times to the point it broke loose from its hinges. I guess that was the Merrier Christmas; at least he left.

The next several months consisted of him being in town again and then out. Mom was working trying to provide for us. She, too, had a side hustle of cleaning people's homes. She also worked for a casino; she was barely scraping by. She had to live off of a server's wages and tips. She had to work every Thanksgiving and some of our Christmases; she had to pick up doubles many times. What little she got made a difference in food or electricity.

He would use this opportunity to weasel his way back in. He would use the excuse he needed to sleep so he could work and give her money. Again, who could blame her? I am sure my mother lived in a state of constant worry and fear most of the time. Even considering the circumstances, she would still be challenging and put on a brave face. She always tried to see the good in him. She thought she could fix him. She would always smile. I love her smile. To this day, I still cannot imagine standing in her shoes. There is no way I could have dealt with what she has.

This is where the mind games and manipulation come in. He was always in on some scheme, always having an alternative motive. This must be why it is so hard for me to trust people; life has hardened me when people show you who they are and believe in them. Years of therapy later, I finally understood that I could trust people. The way I used to see myself was that no one would love me for being me; they would only like me for what they could get from me. Sometimes, my mental state is filled with wondering when the next foot will drop. When is the next person going to hurt me?

My childhood was not horrible all the time. Thankfully, we found some joy in my sister's dog. My god, who knew how much joy and love a dog could bring some sad little, hillbilly, white trash kids. Morgan was a Dalmatian My sister was obsessed with 101 Dalmatians; she went on and on how she wanted one.

Our first Dalmatian was tragically hit by a car; she was taken too soon, and to this day still held dear to my heart. Morgan #2 was purchased to fill our void. She did more than that. She was loving, energetic, and loyal. The one thing we could count on as kids was her. She was the runt of the litter, and I think that is why I felt a closeness with her; I was a runt, and so was she. Even with the odds against us, we still shine.

She was our outside dog. She lived in a large run pen on the other side of our driveway, letting us know when people would pull up and keeping us safe. You could often find me daydreaming inside her raggedy dog house. It was safe, and

I was small enough to fit inside and not be found. Maybe I could have stayed there forever and never be found. Winter was setting in, and it was getting cold. There is nothing like a frigid cold winter day when you live in a pop can.

We always worried about Morgan. She was an outside dog, and it would get cold. She had straw around her house and a heat lamp. I still feel some guilt not being able to keep her safe and warm. I would never let a dog live like that. She was conditioned to the outdoors. I look back on it now, and it doesn't feel kind. I would want so much better for her.

During this month of my tumultuous life, we had to play keep away. Not the child's game, but the adult one. My mom would have to hide my medicine so that the sperm donor would not steal it. I needed the medication. If he got ahold of it, I would be SOL for the next several weeks, which happened several times. When people drastically miss their dosage, they can have crazy, complex, and intolerable mood swings. Why would he care? He didn't give a damn; he wasn't there to pick up the pieces.

He told my sister and me a story of how a dog had frozen to death down the street, and this would probably be Morgan's fate since it was so cold. You can imagine how our little developing brains were entirely traumatized by this; he would wait till we couldn't stand to hear anymore, choking back tears.

He piped up, "There is a way to save her."

We would have done anything to keep our one glimmer of hope alive. We were not aware that the entire time, he had been searching for my hidden medication bottle, as that it was not enough to just traumatize us. He also needed his fix. He told us he needed my pills to stay awake. He would keep her inside and keep a close eye on her so she did not mess anything up in the trailer. He was adamant about getting those pills. We had made a game of finding a new hiding place for the pill bottle each week. He had searched our everyday places and couldn't find them.

I had to save my dog. I could not let her die. I went and got him the pills. They were hidden in my blue flannel shirt pocket in my closet. I was adamant he needed to get her from outside right now so she would not freeze. This man had no intention of going and getting her. I begged, pleaded, and did not shut up till he went out and got her to bring her in. She was an outside dog, had zero discipline, but was warm.

He kept up the charade for a night. He told Mom that out of the kindness of his heart, he got her because we were so upset. He left out the part where he took his child's meds and manipulated us into submission.

However, I have always said karma is a bitch, and she keeps receipts. The sperm donor had dentures. He got into a fight when he was eighteen. This man knocked all of his teeth out. The sperm donor hit back, and the other man fell and hit his head, leading to his death. My father was charged with manslaughter; he was able to get these charges waived. Not sure how though.

Another night when it was cold again, he brought Morgan in to the house. He did not care about the temperature. He wanted more pills from me. This is one reason why we do not negotiate with terrorists ha ha ha.

The sperm donor was zipping all over the place, high on pills; he had not paid a single mind to Morgan. She was several years old, but she still had a puppy mentally, being an outside dog. She decided she needed a new chew toy to pass the time. What better toy than his dentures? She got hold of them. She was chewing on them to the point they were destroyed. Unfortunately, he was mean to her; he beat her and put her back outside. He was evil.

As time went on and I was getting older, he found out that I was not very fond of him.

I was given my first dog around my twelfth birthday. His name was Buddy. He was a golden Pomeranian. Buddy had a ton of hair; he looked like a lion. He was such a beautiful dog. Buddy quickly became my newest confidant and companion. The sperm donor hated that I loved this dog. I loved Buddy more than him.

I had walked down to the store to get him something. In his mind, children were enslaved people who needed to be put to work. He thought he would teach me a lesson. While I was gone, he tied up Buddy to the back porch. He claimed Buddy would not stop barking at him. Buddy did not like to be forcefully thrown into a cage.

I came home to find the sperm donor passed out again on the couch. I searched for Buddy, but I could not find him. I angrily asked, "Where is Buddy?!"

He gathered his thoughts and said, "He is tied up out back."

That was a strange location for him to be. The back of our trailer was right up against a very tall rock wall. I went out to find him. Unfortunately, I only discovered his collar and leash hanging empty from the top of the deck's railing. Buddy had slipped off the side of the back deck Thank God his collar was loose so he could slip out of it; otherwise, he would have hung himself.

I went screaming through the neighborhood to find him. Of course, the sperm donor did not help me look for him; he did not give a crap. He was glad I was hurting He was delighted that my only little happiness was gone. That was the evil that he was. He loved to see people hurt, and it made him feel strong.

I was devastated. Buddy was gone for good; I was sure of it, I thought while crying big tears on the ground. We lived on a bustling state route. There was no way he made it across that road without being hit. I think that was the longest four days I had endured.

A day or two later, a lady entered the little store down the street. She asked if anyone had lost a little dog. She said she was scared that he would get hit, so she opened her car door, and he ran and jumped in. Buddy loved going bye-bye in the car. That was one of his favorite things to do. Thankfully, that is what saved him.

My mom asked her name, and she said, "My name is Angel."

She, indeed, was an angel. If only she knew how much he meant to me, she would see that too. I do feel there was a reason she found him. I will forever be grateful that she brought him home.

I am thankful that I found peace and serenity in the love of my Buddy. This is the reason I love dogs as much as I do. They are always there for you. No matter how the day goes, they still greet you with a wagging tail and a sweet demeanor. Sometimes, a man's best friend can change a whole environment and mindset. I was whole again, thankfully, but this would only be temporary.

Remember the most challenging times in your life. You thought you could never make it through. Then you do. I love the saying, "This too shall pass." I have changed it up a bit now that I am older. I now say, "This too shall pass; it might pass like a kidney stone, but it will pass."

*Chapter Three*

# Darkness With No
# End in Sight

We moved from the slums, the ghetto, where the sperm donor had left us. A picturesque little farm town is where most people want to grow up. Most of the other alternatives were not great. Small farm towns have their secrets too; it is much easier to keep things hush-hush. It's sad to think that some of the best places to live hold so many disturbing secrets. The abuse seems to go on forever.

Okeana is so small, you could hear your neighbors flush their toilets. It was not all bad. there is beauty in living in a close-knit town. People look out for each other; they help keep other people's kids in line and feed other people's kids just for being over there for the day. I am thankful to have made great lifelong connections with the people and families I grew up with.

The small mini-mart where I spent most afternoons purchasing candy on our food stamp card. That is how our Mom tried to make up for some of the shortcomings in our lives.

Halloween was great. Our neighbors were always kind and willing to give us so much candy. Even as we grew older, they would still give us candy. Those are the memories I like to remember; those are the memories that I cherish.

Swimming in the creek, we were like a little gang of neighborhood hillbilly kids. If you needed to find us, you did not pick up a mobile phone or landline. All you had to do was drive by one of the houses and look for the bikes in the front yard. Those were always a dead giveaway.

Some of my worst and fondest memories are of that tiny town.

The sperm donor decided he wanted to go on another bender hiatus, and we were so happy he was gone. My mom was trying to keep food on the table; she couldn't always watch over us how I felt she should.

Perspective is everything. Looking back on our childhood, people would assume it was not that bad. Through the fog of over-medicated and exhausted eyes, did anyone not see it? Children need structure; when it is not present, it is like trying to herd feral cats, with chaos everywhere. When children are left unattended with older siblings, you assume the younger kids are being cared for, but how well do you know? Do you trust your older children to guide and protect your younger and innocent children?

Leaving kids for several hours after school does not seem like a lot of time, but sometimes that is more than enough time. I remember being in the third grade when one of my teachers had to drive me home. I was forgotten. I was so thankful that she took me home. I was incredibly embarrassed at the same time. She was one of my favorite teachers; she was patient and kind. I think her name was Mrs. Theme or something like that. She had to drive me to the dilapidated trailer with torn-off skirting and trash strung out through the overgrown, grassy yard. I am unsure why I was not picked up that day after school. I had to stay after for some additional help.

I was left at the school several times with no one to pick me up. I am assuming this is where a lot of my abandonment issues have come from. The squeaky wheel gets the oil. I stopped asking for help, for love, for care; Mom had so much on her plate as it was. I was only going to add more.

Over the next several months, I sank into a lonely, super-dark place. I had very little in common with my siblings. They loved sports and yelled at the TV. I will still never understand that concept. It was me and my doggie all by ourselves most of the time, with no structure, normalcy, routine, just darkness. This mindset is such a vulnerable state for a little boy. Not heard, not understood, different, weird, emotional, sensitive.

Looking back on this, I felt like I was drowning. I felt like I was standing on my tip toes and could barely keep my mouth from filling with water, just gasping for air. Again, more darkness. Why am I alone? I must be the problem. Would it be better if I wasn't here?

Sadly, these thoughts would continue to run rampant through my mind for years. No one would ever know. I put a smile on my face and flash my pretty blue eyes, and no one would ever know. I painstakingly got very good at this.

My eyes were the key—big, bright baby blue eyes. I do love my eyes. They are gorgeous, and I am blessed that my parents' DNA gave them to me. Almost everyone would compliment them. If I wanted something from anyone, I could generally get it. My shy demeanor with my stunning blue eyes and porcelain skin did the trick every time. Looking for any attention that could come my way for someone to see and notice me. I did not realize that I would come to despise them.

In the sea of darkness, a new light would finally appear from a close family friend. People didn't go out of their way for me. Some tried, but I assumed my shy demeanor wasn't worth trying to force conversations from me. But he made a point to see me. He made a point to hear me. He consistently went out of his way for me. I had never had anyone other than my mother who would go above and beyond for me. Making sure I understood things and asking me if I needed help. Helping me understand some of my homework that consistently I would fall behind in. Helping me understand social cues.

I could sit and watch him play video games all day; it was a total vibe that just existed. I think I saw him as a protector, a brother, a father. I am not sure what the pull was, but it was undeniably amazing to feel special. I could ask for anything, and he always obliged.

Wow, is this what friends do for each other?

He was more family than my actual family. He looked out for me, not letting anyone pick on me. He would help educate me with all the things I never understood. I felt closeness. I felt normal for the first time in my life. I finally fit in. I was a cool kid; someone had my back. He was a pillar I could lean on. He would help me get dressed, ensuring my zipper and button on my pants were always fastened. He helps me tie my shoes. He lets me sit by or near him whenever he is around. He was cool.

He was caring, or so I thought. Alternative motives started to sneak in on our friendship. Small things started to change; it went from super accommodating to no accommodation. At the time, I felt I had done something to make him feel cold, and I could not understand it. I would rack my brain repeatedly, trying to figure out what I did. Then, out of nowhere, it was right back to where it was. Our friendship was back again.

This mental and emotional abuse would continue for the next several weeks, leading into months. It felt like violent emotional whiplash. Sometimes, things would be fine. Then other times, he would put me down in front of my brothers or friends. I was back into emotional whiplash. It was like what I felt from the sperm donor. I felt it from my family, too. I just wanted them to see me for me. I wanted to receive some of the love that I constantly gave. Again, the darkness surfaced, but this time, it was detrimental to my physical and mental health.

I wish there was a different outcome for this part of the story; no one expects their life to spiral. We would never want a parent or child to go through it.

The emotional abuse and power struggle are referred to as "grooming." Grooming entails building a relationship, often to gain trust or control. This can be seen in social, psychological, or even criminal contexts where someone may engage in manipulative behaviors to establish a connection with another person. I was not aware of this term until much later in life.

Context is everything when referring to this term. When I wanted something, I had to do something to get it. His kindness became a vicious cycle that would continue for years: deeper manipulations, hurt, and darkness. I was being molested. How quickly this turned. It's taken me several decades to come to term with this. I felt this was my fault. I thought I had to do these things to keep my sister safe; if he was doing them to me, he might not hurt her. She was my sole worry now. I could turn my brain off. I could make my body to be numb to fight through such horrid acts.

He was several years older than me. I think I was nine to thirteen, some of which is a blur of blocking out what happened to me. If I stopped him or made a scene, he would tell everyone it was my fault. I had a higher pitch voice and played with Barbies. Who would believe me? Here was this macho sixteen-year-old that everyone liked. Then you have me, a sensitive, emotional little boy whose mannerisms were more feminine.

Several years later, I would come to the terms of my identity: I was gay. It makes it all better because clearly, I liked it. How people can overlook that much pain is beyond me. The story and narrative that would soon come to life is that I wanted it; I was the problem, not him. This story would be used as leverage for years—some by him, some by my family. My family knew what was happening, but no one thought of helping. They let someone hurt me. They allowed someone to strip every bit of innocence from me. I should have been helped. I was a child.

This is when my insecurities started to root subconsciously; the insecurities that haunted me for years to come. The statistics are alarming that little boys cannot be harmed, or they need to toughen up. Whatever the situation. It is wrong. It's why boys never come forward to find the help they need. They choose to bury it so deeply.

It's tough to put these words to paper; it's something I have forced down so profoundly. I'm not too fond of this being a part of my story, but unfortunately, it is. I had not thought of this pain in years—not until my niece reached the age of ten. Then it all came back to me like a ton of bricks. I cannot even imagine someone hurting her. I would gladly sit in prison with a smile on my face to retaliate if anyone even attempted to harm her. It was then that I realized I could accept this happening to me because it was me. However, I was a child at the time. He knew better; they knew better.

The individuality of how someone's brain is shaped from trauma is quite complex; you never know when that ugly trauma will rear its head and lash out. You behave in a manner of protection. Diving deep into why you do the things you do is a truly freeing feeling. Let go of the darkness and look in the mirror when you cannot find the light. You might be the guiding light you have always needed.

I want to leave this chapter on a good note. It was not your fault; be kind to yourself; they did that to you. You did not allow them to do it to you. If you are reading this and struggle with any traumas, please consider asking for help. My biggest regret was not asking for help much sooner. You do not have to do it alone; you do not have to carry this burden for decades. Love yourself and allow yourself to be free of all of the trauma. Those traumas may have built you, but they are not you. It is the freest you will ever be. You can and will make it through this. Please reach out to anyone for help. Do not be ashamed. You have nothing to be ashamed of.

This is not the end of your story. Merely only the beginning. The healing starts now.

*Chapter Four*

# Smash it all to Pieces

Time seemed to fly by, through the treacherous years of my life. What is even the point? Being stuck in such a hard place numbs you, keeps you cold, and keeps you from growing. These are the times I can describe when the walls started to close in on me. How much can one child take?

I started to take some control of my life, only to be dropped and kicked right back to the bottom. It's like climbing a mountain; the snow keeps pushing you back. No matter how hard you try, how much you climb, and how much distance you cover, you are still consistently in the same spot.

The mind-altering meds that had been forced on me for so long—I decided I would remove those shackles from me. It felt like an explosion had gone off when I finally came out of the withdrawal period of these meds. Everything seemed so much clearer. I felt again that I could eat; there Trenton was for the first time in so many years of him being gone. There he was! It is wild to think I lived in such a dead state for so long. I had lost every bit of my personality to those meds that kept me numb.

Puberty and hormones came back, and they were raging. Shifting my mind into more confusion. I found some peace, and I could put some of the darkness behind me. I loved me again. I could finally start to love again. I was a ladies' man who dated several ladies throughout my teens. I never had a problem keeping them near me. I was walking the path that was chosen for me all those years ago: meet a girl, fall in love, go to college, get married, buy a house, and have kids. I appreciate all the people who helped shape this journey of my life.

You find someone who is truly amazing; they love you unconditionally. Wow, okay, this has to be it; this is what everyone rages about, the intoxicating feeling of young love and infatuation. Or is this another trick to get hurt?

I started building the walls higher before these relationships even took off. It is so hard to reshape behaviors when you are subconsciously doing it. Keeping walls up means you never have to hurt or feel pain again. What they forgot to tell you is you also keep love out. You will only mature to the level of mental capacity that you allow. You do not grow—sure, in age, but emotional growth is halted. You harden, grow cold. You are charismatic, but you have never felt so alone. You have tons of friends, yet you are still alone.

Following the pre-constructed path is incredibly lonely, to the point of deafening. You work hard to build relationships. Work diligently to make friends, but do they ever get to see you? The real you, the raw you. The ugly you. Nope, we put on that happy smile and keep moving forward. Brush all those emotions to the side; you cannot feel those, you have to push them down. You do not want to be called "sensitive" anymore. The minute you try to articulate those emotions, you are labeled again. Push them down, and keep it moving.

You look for love in all the wrong places to hopefully find your space in this universe. The abuse continues in the manner of emotional abuse. Your family needs to control and manipulate you for as long as they can.

I'm not loving you for being you.

They love you for the image, they use love for their

alternative motives. They don't want you, but they don't want someone else to love you. The deafening, demeaning, comments that are hurled at you daily, you start to believe them. It is sad those comments became the normal of my life. If it were a good day, fewer of them would happen. However, if it was a bad day, they seemed to never stop. I cannot tell you how many times I was labeled stupid, retard, dumb, fag, sissy, pussy, and queer. Those were just some of the everyday words I would hear repeatedly from my family. The minute they did not get their way, the words would be hurled at me again.

I was looking for more avenues of escape. I just wanted them to be proud of me. I tried everything to earn their love and acceptance. I had a girlfriend whom I loved, but she wasn't good enough. She was a brown girl. Ah, the never-ending I can't make them happy.

I did find someone I had cared for. I would hide in the safety of her love for years. She was one reason I could fall in love and see what that meant. Hiding at her home was such a foreign concept. Her mom was also a single mom. She was always there for her daughter. Like, there for her. Like, I've got your back, I'll stab anyone for you there.

Her mom was so attentive. She took me under her wing to care for me. She showed me what normalcy is. Their home wasn't filled with torture, broken things, and chaos. She filled it with love. That girl and her mom showed me what unconditional love was. They loved me, all of me— the hurt and numb me, the ugly me, the stupid me. Being in this environment was so far from what I was raised in. Mine was watching out because someone was about to throw something. Pay attention. At any minute, you might need to duck. You'll get hit in the face or kicked in the ribs into the stove out of nowhere. My home life was alarmingly unpredictable. This home was the first home where I felt safe for the first time in sixteen years. Is this what home should feel like?

Both supported me; up until this point in my life, I had never been supported. Unconditionally, genuinely, wholeheartedly supported. What is this? Do people care about you and support you with no alternative motive? It seems like a trick; I will add another brick to the wall just to be safe.

The thing about people who will, no matter what, be there for you, is that they will keep on climbing that wall. They will hang there for years, with no qualms or complaints, just climbing away and supporting you. It doesn't matter how high you build that wall; they will still hang out even when you add the next layer. They will climb to that layer. They will graciously wait for a hole or crack to open up so they can say, "Hi." Never to push your boundaries. Just trying to understand what those boundaries are.

For them, waiting for that small glimmer of hope of being on the other side of that wall. They want to be on the other side of all that pain. They see how good of a person you are, how great you can be, and how loving you will be. To support the broken you, the raw you, the hurt you, and still look you in the face, say three simple words with extreme impact: "I love you."

Unfortunately, building walls leads to casualties; you can only give so much of yourself to someone when you remember why that wall exists. You push away love, a love that some people search their whole life for; it is easier to hide behind the wall. You keep building. You have to surround yourself with the wall on four sides, which goes higher and higher.

It eventually comes to a box, built to keep people out, but it's also keeping you in, like a prison cell. There is no light, just cold, dark walls. What do you do? You try again, round and round, on a hamster wheel. You are constantly spinning away, chasing nothing but emptiness. More failed relationships. They just don't fit. You find no excuse to escape it. You start hurting people unintentionally. More casualties, more hurt.

The walls have collapsed in on me. With no way out. The air is thin. The darkness has now consumed me. This time, it's way different; it's intentional, it's catastrophic, it's calm, it's peaceful, it's home. When you are pushed to the brink of complete and utter collapse, it is hard to see the good in the world; the darkness consumes you. This is your emotional roller coaster, the one you built, the one you allowed. The problem is, you are perfectly fine riding it up and down until it calmingly comes to the top, and the last glimmer of light slowly goes out.

Where did the track go? It is gone all of it. The end is near.

When you have gone down the path with no end in sight, you are beaten, bruised, and exhausted. It eats away at you; your life starts to play back all the pain, turmoil, and trauma, all rearing their heads, taking chunks out of you after each passing memory. The answer is simple. Would anyone even miss me if I was gone? This world is going to be better off when I am gone.

Suicidal thoughts had taken over my brain. The world seemed much more tolerable in this place. I arrived at this place abruptly. It sneaks up on you. Like a thief in the night. The darkness does not care about your age or gender; darkness does not discriminate. It does not care that you are a lost boy. When it comes, it breaks the door off the hinges. It will not let you go until it takes you as a whole. I would show all of them what it is like living in the hell that was my life; you tried to break me, and you succeeded. I had it planned out.

I had the day and the location. I would get my truck up to a high speed and red line that little Ford Ranger. It would sound like a hot rod, screaming through the streets of Okeana. I would slam it into the pole that was located across the street from the home where I was constantly pushed out. Maybe then they would see me, and I would teach them a lesson in suffering.

The day had come. I had been alone for so long. Reaching these lengths in life is not scary; you are just at peace. The peace of never hurting again, never being tormented or tortured, never being used and abused, just at peace. Depression is a terrible place. It is twisted mind games, it is revolutions, and it is hurt.

Goodbye, cruel world. I never want to see you again.

Then a flood of light, beaming light, blinding light. It shined so damn bright it felt like it would burn my retinas. She stepped in, she threw the darkness back. She kicked the door off of its hinges, rebuilt that door, and sealed it with more steel than you have ever seen. She picked me up, brushed me off, and hugged me.

She said, "You won't ever have to be alone. You are enough. You deserve all the love you are trying to give. I will hold you up for as long as it takes; I am not taking no for an answer. There is so much more to life, and you have so much more to live." And then: "Now put your big girl panties on and deal with it!"

This lady saved me. She came in when I needed her most. She read through all the numbness and pain. She body-slammed that wall till she could get over it. She is why I am alive today.

People come into your life as a blessing or a lesson. Pay attention; you will never know how badly you need someone until you have nothing left. Chari saved my life. She was my ex's mother. She did not abandon me even though I broke her daughter's heart and shattered it into pieces. She saw my bruised and battered heart; she stepped in and took over. She did not have to. She stepped up her Momma bear mode.

To all the Charis, you are someone's light in their darkness. Do not ever let it burn out. The simplest of gestures can change someone's entire outlook on life. To truly understand someone's darkness, you must go through it yourself.

Thank you, irrevocably and undeniably, for saving our lives.

If you are struggling, please listen to me. Don't suffer alone. There are many resources to help you. You are enough, you are seen, you don't have to be alone. Reach out. Stop the suffering today if you can take anything from this book. Please consider this statement.

Chari said to me, "You have so much to live. This is just a small roadblock in your journey. Your journey starts now. People can only affect you if you allow them. I am your physical proof. If I can make it out, you can too. You are someone's light, even though you are in darkness. I see you and know that I want you to win."

*Chapter Five*

# Closets Are Meant
# for Clothes, not People

I think some of us can relate. High school is great, but for others, it can be some of the worst times of your life. My time in high school was not great. I am truly super fortunate that I had a few people in my corner through these tough times. I am not sure how I graduated. I think I missed seventy-six days my senior year.

There is a plus to ADHD. I can hyper focus for hours on end if I am super dedicated to it. Leaving grade school was a valley and peak moment for me. I was bullied, I didn't understand things as quickly as other kids. Here we go again; I was cast to the side. I was home schooled for a year in the fifth grade, then attended a private Christian school the following year.

My education was all over the place. I read and spelled at a fourth-grade level in the six grade. I never finished tasks, a lot of incomplete work and essays. I was the charity at the Christian school. We could not afford the tuition. Some parents showed pity on me. They helped build a scholarship for me. My mother worked at the school to get a discount for tuition.

I know how the other kids felt about me. I know how they looked at me. I was the poor kid again. Just desperately trying to fit in. I was different. There was not anyone like me. The short-lived schooling and somewhat of a focused education would stop. My mom would have to leave the school; we could not afford to go there. I would have to start school in the fall back into public school.

My peers, the ones who remembered me, were excelling far past me. That year was rough, especially being unmedicated. My education was never of importance. I did not learn like my siblings. It was easier to overlook me. You learn to stop asking for help. Did anyone even notice?

My high school years consisted of taking my parents back and forth to doctor appointments. I was the taxi. I was the one child who was reliable, and I put up the least amount of fight. The squeaky wheel gets the oil. This is so true. When you stop asking for help, you just accept and believe it for what it is. No one cares.

I was able to scrape by in high school. I knew something was different about me, I just couldn't put my finger on it. Sure, other men check each other out. They may not admit it but they do. I just felt I was envious of how other guys looked. I admired them. I, at the time, wanted to be them. Tough, macho, chiseled. One can dream, right?

This is where things start to pick up and change for me. Not only did Chari smash my walls to pieces, but she also had to rebuild my structure to put me on top. First, you don't get to feel sorry for yourself; the harsh truth is no one cares and works harder. She instilled hard work into me.

Nothing in this life is free, so get up and work for it. This life owes you nothing. You want something go and get it. You will find a way, not an excuse. When you want something bad enough you will find the way.

I had a bad day. It's a bad day, not a bad life. Those words will help you through. You will get what you want out of this life the minute you realize that no one is coming to save you. Nothing will be handed to you, and you must take the deepest dive of your life; you must work, work, and work. You must figure out who you are and what you want to achieve in this mindset.

After one of the more challenging spots in my life, I understood some things: I was different. Yep, different. No matter how hard I tried to fit in the box, it didn't work. It's because humans are not meant to be in a box; they are not meant to be labeled. I am Trenton. Just Trenton. I have no idea why anyone would want to fit in with the crowd. They are all the same—Typical, Standard, Basic. I never want to be described in those words. I am pretty sure the great Dr. Seuss said, "Why fit in when you are born to stand out." I have lived a lot of my life by this motto. Guess what? You're different; that's what makes you, YOU.

Understanding and accepting the taboo of being gay at the time was trying and taxing. I did not want to be gay; hell, I would have never chosen that life in a million years. Living in a rural area, there are not many people like you. I think there were three gay people, to be exact, and they were out and proud. I was jealous of them; they owned it and did not let anyone tell them anything different.

In some ways, I am a coward. I kept my secret from everyone. I did not have the strength to feel the pressures of yet another title and label. Everyone's journey is different; you must face it alone. One colossal help was Chari's continued support. I was told there was nothing I could do or say to make her look at me differently and love me any less. There is support. That is what people should do to help you.

Once I decided I had come to terms with this little bump in the road, I kicked down that closet door and came out impeccably dressed to impress and ready to manifest. I started to understand what it was like to live authentically through my own eyes. I let go of the judgment. I let go of what I thought my life was supposed to be, and I started looking at the life I wanted.

Remember when I told you people come crashing into your life? They are either a blessing or a lesson. Again, another one, BAM! it's like a Mack truck.

We didn't have social media at the time and the internet was hard to get to, listening to the god-awful sound of a dial-up modem. If you know, you know. At the beginning of 2008, came Myspace, where you could show the most incredible version of yourself on a web page, and way more customizable than Facebook.

I think my username was Pimp Kewl? I was so cool. . . Ha! It's nice to look back and laugh.

I got an instant message—yes, that was what it was called before you all called it DM—not knowing that message would be one of my biggest lessons and blessings at the same time. When you come to terms with yourself, you unlock a world you never knew existed. You start to look at life differently; everything you thought you knew, everything that was important to you, doesn't suit you any longer.

The message was from a guy named Bryan. A tall, dark, and handsome guy. He had eyes that would make you melt. A body to match and a bad-boy personality with a bow on top. Hubba hubba, if you will. This man took me by surprise, took my breath away, lit my world and body on fire! Holy hell, so now this all makes sense! This is what I had been dreaming of my entire life!

He fit the bill. We were casual and having fun, and both pretty young. The intoxicating love that quickly transpired was surreal and out of this world. The passion, the lust, staying in bed all day enamored. He took me to the movies. Talk about a dream guy. He made me feel so special. We were both broke and so young, but that didn't matter. For the first time, I got what I wanted. I was not looking for it; it just gravitated toward me.

What else can I accomplish with this mindset? The happiness. The safety. The peace.

In business, you must roll with the punches, and I was headed for a big sucker punch. As quickly as this relationship blossomed, it smacked to the floor like a sack of potatoes. This relationship would go up in flames on Christmas Eve.

Devasted, shattered, and heartbroken, like really broken, like broken into a billion pieces. Why would this happen to me? Why? I have finally gotten out of the darkness. Here comes another blow, another hit, another disappointment.

I sat with this feeling for a long time, trying to figure out what had gone wrong, what had changed, and why he would just cast me to the side like discarded trash so effortlessly. Even heavier insecurities crept in. This is where my world would turn and lock into place. They do not love you. They only love what they can get from you. This thought haunted me until my mid-thirties.

His excuses were superficial at best, covering the real issue. Remembering it takes one to know one, I could see and feel his hurt and his demons; sometimes, that is how life goes, and everything eventually comes to an end. You must take the good times when they come. Hold onto them, sit in the happy, be in the now, and be present. Grab it tight and keep it till it fades away.

The next several years were littered with ups and downs, a few failed relationships, and more lessons, thankfully. The lesson I am trying to prove here is that through the ups and downs, rock bottom will teach you lessons that mountain tops never will. How does the dirt feel? It should feel like shit. It feels terrible. I would rather feel beautiful cobblestone streets lined with perfect trees. Or a Tuscany patio overlooking a vineyard. Or slow rock of waves against my beautiful boat in the middle of summer.

Those feelings hang onto them. Store them away but keep them close. When you are at rock bottom, you can only go up. You have to transform your mind and put out to the universe what you want from this life. No one is going to give it to you. It would help if you were determined and ready to grab this life by its balls and run ahead. If you hesitate, you will fail. Mind over matter. You must rewire and train your brain for what you need and want it to do.

Understanding one's true self and believing in yourself is the first step. Why do you deserve to sit at the table with the decision-makers? Sit yourself down and write it down. It does not have to be super thought out. Write down your dreams, write down your goals, write down your wants. What do you want people to say at your funeral? What do you want to be remembered for? Those questions will get you started on your way.

Success is not given; it is earned. Do you deserve it? Then prove it. Get it all down on paper and put it up in your home. Keep looking at it every day. Watch your mindset start to transform and leave the old you behind. Stay true to yourself, and success will come. Try not to harp on the low points or failures; they will be monumental in carving the new journey.

# Chapter Six

# These Hours Will Be the Death of Me

I was in college full time. I was working full time. My days consisted of working from 5am to 1pm, Monday through Friday, at a sandwhich, then going to school three to five nights a week, from 6pm to 10pm. I filled in part-time watching the front desk of the college; my weekends weren't mine. I worked for a catering company on Saturday mornings. Most days, it was a double, then back into the catering company on Sunday morning. This was fine. I was getting an education toward something I wanted: Design.

You have to put in the hours, especially when you realize no one is coming to save you. You had to get the money when the money was good. That sacrifice was one of my more challenging lessons; I would not always take a shift at the catering company. Why? I was tired.

Get over it. You will be exhausted. You are not setting yourself up for success if you are not tired. Do you want an easy street? Or easier street? Want to kill motivation quickly? Get comfortable. Being comfortable is the biggest motivation killer. If you are lucky enough to be comfortable you should still hustle like the electricity will be turned off this week.

When you get to this step in the process, and you think

you have made it. Start again, only this time you cannot make your car payment. Keep pushing. You will love this level of uncomfortable, it trains your mind to keep hustling. Over and over.

Some of the best classes I took in high school that I found extremely helpful were Intro to Business and Personal Finance. Those classes taught me how to structure a business and introduced me to managing money. It's crazy to me that those classes were considered electives. Like why the hell are we not teaching kids this as required learning?

I was following a path that I thought would set me up for success. Go to college you have to get an education. Then get a good job working for a big company. They have all the perks, PTO, 401k and a pension. That is the only way to be successful. That was the drive; I wanted to be successful. That is the path that was drilled into my brain. We do not challenge society; we have to go with the masses. Keep on working. Clock those hours in for years to obtain a retirement. Retirement seemed impossible. I had no clue how people did it.

Then the economy collapsed in 2009. I went from making okay money down to minimum wage. Overnight. The catering company took a big hit and scaled back its operations, laying off most of its people. Hi, I'm most of the people. Then, through all this, I was accused of theft from my job at the sandwich place. ; I am meticulous about money. I always organized all the bills in my register, keeping them face up. Even with no video evidence, I was forced to quit. I was the poor kid, a label that would follow me. I was lacking and not as successful as other people my age, so that automatically made me a thief, right? Wrong.

There are two things I hate most in this world. One is a liar and the other is a thief. You can call me any name in the book, and I will not flinch, however if you call me a liar or a thief, those are fighting words. Those are character assassinations. Being a poor child, you will always be accused of being one or the other or both. I will defend my name and character until I am blue in the face. No one ever defended me; I had to defend me. The better part of this story is that they eventually found the thief, and they were surprised it was not me. Do you think I got an apology? Do you think I was offered my job back. Nope. That did not matter to anyone.

Again, no one would save me; I had to save me.

I started working for a temp agency, trying to take my career in different directions, doing anything to bring in money. My boyfriend at the time was the farthest thing from supportive. I had to work. I had to keep my mind toward the goal. You should pay attention to the company you hold. It can be detrimental to your journey. I learned this the hard way. You know me, beating to the tune of my own drum. I have a type; trust me, I know how to pick them.

Through hard work and determination, I was able to maintain a job and keep my school schedule in check. I was making ten dollars an hour. I could barely afford school, even with the loans. Oh, you know you cannot purchase a home, but you can take out thousands of dollars in school loans without anyone batting an eye. They don't explain to you that these loans will eventually cripple you. SCAM. Student funding is a joke; it is predatory and throws you into debt. Pay attention to loan terms read the fine print. Do not sign anything without reading all of it first. You will likely get the pleasure of paying off those loans for the rest of your life.

Some moments in your life will be the most profound things you will ever have to go through. April 18, 2011, was that day for me.

It started like any other day. I went to work again I was on the outs with my ex; my other man-friend met me after work that day he dumped me. Again, I was completely blindsided. Did I mention I have a type?

Heading home, I had a weird flood of emotion. It was like a rush of heat. It was strange; I had never felt this before. The feelings were super alarming. It was not from being dumped. I did not cry because I did not care. I was always waiting for them to hurt me. They all eventually walk out and leave me. This is the cycle I have chosen to accept: an unfortunate cycle.

I made it home, where I was renting a room from my other ex. Can you say toxic behavior? Such great environments I put myself in. I was scanning through Facebook on my Blackberry bold cell phone, which I couldn't afford. I quickly checked the newsfeed, and there was a small article was about a local girl from Ross High School, the school I had graduated from, who had been killed in a car accident. Unfortunately, lots of loss was coming from that area. We all were young learning to drive and also learning how to play with phones while driving. We were distracted by the new cell phones everyone had to have.

I closed Facebook without a thought in mind. Five minutes later, my phone rang. It was my mom. I did not answer; we were not on the greatest of terms at the time. She called back immediately, which was strange. This time, I answered. My mother's voice rang out, her words will forever be a permanent mark in my brain: "Your sister was killed today in a car accident."

I said, "That is not funny. Why would you say this?"

She said, "It is true."

The uncontrollable jolts of emotions that flooded me are ones I hope you will never feel in your life. The air from your lungs is stripped from you. The entire world stops in one instant. Your heart feels like it is beating so fast, that it will explode. The pain that shoots through your body is one you will never ever forget.

Tell the people who are most important to you that you love them. Every single time you can. You have no idea when that might be your last chance to say it to them. Tarrista was my younger sister. She was twenty. I was twenty-one. She was the only person I kept close to in my family. She was the only reason I was around them.

She and I were inseparable. People thought we were twins since we looked alike. She was a stunning blonde bombshell with piercing blue eyes. She was incredible and drop-dead gorgeous. She could walk into any room and turn heads. She had the personality everyone dreams of. She was an athlete, a good student, and book smart. She got book smarts; I got street smarts.

I recalled the last conversation I had with her. It had been four days prior. She wanted to see me, and I had to work. That was one of many times I couldn't see her due to my insane working schedule. That is one of my biggest regrets in life. I was harping on her. She had gotten a B-plus in one of her college courses. She was an A student. She did not really have to apply herself she soaked up knowledge like a sponge. She could easily blow through a week's worth of projects in just a few hours. She was really gifted in that department.

I wanted better for her. I wanted her to get the life she had always wanted, never asking anyone for anything. She would have kiddos who would not have to overcome their childhood with two loving parents. I was hard on her because she deserved better. I shielded her for so long from the dysfunction that was our life. I told her she needed to get her head straight and not let the boys lead her astray.

I told her I loved her when I got off the phone, not knowing that would be the last time we ever spoke. Even now, it's getting harder to remember her voice. I wish I had a recording of it. Her laugh was contagious; her energy always influenced the room. Everyone wanted to be around her. She was set to go to Paris in the fall to teach English to French children. Can you imagine what her life should have been like? She was the light in the darkness.

The emotions continued to consume me. It is like having your organs ripped from your body. There is a hole in my heart that never goes away. If you ever have to wonder why someone is grieving so long, consider yourself very lucky that you don't understand it.

We had plans. Our kids would grow up together. She already had her kids' names picked out; she incorporated all our middle names into her children's names. She was my person, the only sibling who had my back through thick and thin. We were there for each other. We knew each other better than we knew ourselves.

Her life was ripped from her at a moment's notice. Her body was burnt, and we had a closed casket. I was not able to get the closure I needed. I wanted to say goodbye.

No one prepares you for this kind of pain and loss. I never thought that I would have to pick out her funeral casket before her wedding dress. You see your parents getting older and know the inevitable will happen one day. Not this one. She was ripped from my life. This was my first huge, big lesson of actual loss. How cruel life can be. How all of your life can be taken in an instant. The world can be a cruel dark place. When we are young, we think we are invincible; that won't ever happen to me. Until one day, your arrogance is shocked right out of you. Never say never. You will never know when the universe decides to punch your ticket.

# Chapter Seven

# The Odds Aren't Even
# in the Ballpark

Such loss comes with a cost; this one stopped me dead in my tracks and put me on my ass. You start to evaluate your life, what is essential, what will matter to you at the end of the day. All the money in the world could never alter my mind after this tragic loss. I would gladly trade my life for hers; she was good. Why do bad things happen to good people? You think of all the shitbags you have met in your life, and this young lady, so full of life, has her life ripped from her. I would give anything to speak to her one more time, anything to dance with her one more time, anything to go cruising at night in Okeana with the radio blaring on a hot summer night. Those are the essential things.

As bad as you want the world to stop turning, it does not. My ex, whom I was living with at the time, said he was going to do right by me. That he was going to change, he had made an enormous mistake. Breaking things off with me was stupid and he wanted to prove that to me. He spoke of marriage, a future of normal where I didn't have to do all the heavy lifting.

Your perspective gets very clear when your sister's friends offer their condolences. The things that matter in life are not things at all. The most important thing is your time. I no longer tell people to get me Christmas gifts; I am blessed with more than enough. I ask them to take me to dinner to sit and enjoy each other's company. The greatest gift you can ever give is your time. Make sure you are using it sparingly.

If you had one day left to live, how would you spend it? Please write it down. Make that your goal. That is what you will be working toward.

The next several weeks were blurry; the alcohol crept in. I was drinking more than ever. I had called into my job for only three days to attend her funeral. When I returned to work, I was greeted with one week back to find out I was being let go because I had missed too much time from work. Like WTF? Gee. Thanks. Now, as a business owner, I cannot believe a company would do this to someone.

Yet again, I was scrambling to get my life back together. College came to a screeching halt, considering I was making ten dollars an hour at the temp agency. That was not going to happen. I had to beg a friend of mine for a job at Wendy's Old-Fashioned Hamburgers. I was making eight dollars an hour. I had started these trying times at eighteen dollars an hour and now I was making eight. How quickly we can fall.

I tried to keep my head above water. I tried to look at the positives. Well, at least I had someone who had changed and was understanding. My boyfriend at the time was primarily supportive. We had dated for over a year. He also had hidden agendas. He was not attracted to me, for reasons he could not explain; I was a solid eight then, and he was more like a rough two. The arguments seemed to have ended. We were getting along for the most part. I was in a drunken state of grief. It crippled me as a human.

We decided to go out for drinks. He was acting weird while drinking. He was not big with phones. He normally was never on it. I was always the DD. This night I had been drinking, but I decided to drive home anyway. We made it home in one piece; I cannot for the life of me tell you how we did.

The normal routine sets in. He passed out on our couch, lying near me. Strangely, that night, his phone was permanently attached to his hand. I had never gone through a phone before. All I did was click it. There was a message dated 4/25/2011, sent from a random ugly guy: "I thought you had a boyfriend?"

My ex replied: "It's fine. This will be our little secret."

He cheated on me three days after my sister's funeral. I was mourning. He used this to his advantage. What kind of person does this? Oh I forgot, I have a type of choosing emotionally unavailable men.

All at once, I had slid back into such a state of sadness, loneliness, and emptiness. I guess this is what I got for trying to better myself, wanting to be better for myself, trying to rise from the depths of extreme poverty. The odds never seemed to be in my favor. Shit, when have they ever been in my favor?

Bitterness started setting in, a fresh emotion of bitterness. I should settle in for this new normalcy. I should throw in the towel and call it a day...

These stories are hard. They are harsh, they are ugly. These stories have shaped me to be who I am today. These stories created a lot of great qualities for me. When you are in the thick of it, it is hard to see past it. Reflecting on the past is super beneficial; it keeps you grounded, it keeps you humble. Keep moving forward. This, too, shall pass.

Whenever I think of throwing in the towel, I hang on just a little longer for something to change. Remember, everything in life is temporary; your life can change instantly. One thing consistently rings true despite all the pain, loss, and traumas: Dragging yourself into a positive mindset will be a surefire way of getting you back on course, where you need to be. When times are more challenging, you must look at it this way: everything happens for a reason. Is this a lesson or a blessing? Sometimes, we can't see everything happening for a reason, and sometimes, we are not meant to.

The next several months were filled with drinking benders, met with more emptiness. I tried to go back to college. Another SCAM. I could take out as many loans as I needed, but I didn't finish two weeks, and it will cost me 1,500.00 dollars out of pocket. Remember that fine print I told you to read; they like to make these details fine print. Well, my dreams just went up in flames.

In times like these, it's important to look around and see who is actually there for you. Like really there for you. I was fortunate enough to have a friend that had my back. Even when it wasn't deserved. The one I could lean on. Another friend that would keep me sane, another friend to save my life. Those are your people. You might fall astray, but you will always gravitate toward the ones who you are supposed to be with.

I was working at Wendy's, making eight dollars an hour. That number wasn't even feasible. My ex was making sure to slide me no favors, especially since I outed his scheming ways. Sadly, I would not get back on track anytime soon, I and should accept that this was as good as it will get. Nowhere to turn.

I had an idea. Since my life was already in flames, let's try dating again. Off to the app I went. Surfing the web for Mr Charming. I got a message from a guy. He ended up being my new chapter, for now. He was kind, understanding, and supportive. I was not sure of this kind of person because he was not my type. However, considering my track record, I realized I should probably do the opposite of what I usually do and hope it works out. Thankfully, it did.

For once, I had a glimmer of hope. I had a bit of restored hope. He could look over my past, see my pain, and lift me like no one had ever done. There were so many crazy things that I could not believe. For one, his birthday was the same as my sister's. What are the odds? We had tons of weird little connections like that. We seemed to have hit it off. He made sure I was taken care of and he genuinely protected me.

He also dealt with his fair share of mess from me. Drunken breakdowns, me starting a fight with him for no reason; he would not even yell at me. He told me, "You have had too many people do that to you, and no matter how hard you try to push me away, I will not do that to you. You deserve better."

Wow. I deserve better.

That was the first time someone had said this to me.

This newfound hope came with its set of challenges while in mourning; I could easily overlook those tiny little red flags. He meant well. He was very kind, and I am so thankful he was there to lean on while I was in mourning. Honestly, I think he was put in my path, by my sister. She knew I would need someone to just be there for me. Be kind to me. Support me, even when it was not deserved.

The universe started to tilt for me once more. Things started to look up. I started a new job rolling burritos. I no longer had to work in the hood till 3am. It certainly was not the safest of areas. I should have gotten out sooner rather than later.

I worked on trying to re-establish my mindset and goals. I did a deeper dive into myself. I wanted more for myself. First things first, I started to sober the hell up, and started looking through clear eyes again. I had come out of my eight-month drinking bender. For the first time in a long time, I was like, "Good god, Trenton, wake the hell up. You have gotten distracted again."

My relationship was okay, for the most part. He had his demons, but one thing I could not overlook was complacency. He was satisfied with his life. He wanted no more or no less. We did not have a bad life by any means. It was just a difference of opinion. He was set with his life, and I was engaged to him. I was screaming inside. I had no business being engaged to anyone. I was pushing through the emotions, like I always do. I do believe he was put in my path for a reason. He really was a great guy, I just subconsciously overlooked lots of things I would have never overlooked had I not been in mourning.

I was no gem by any stretch of the imagination. I did things I am not proud of. The last thing I ever wanted was to hurt him. I truly do owe him my life. I am not sure if he had not been a part of it that I would be sitting in this chair writing this book. I will forever be grateful for what he did for me.

I did find out a little bit later that he was still married. They were separated, but there was zero effort from either party's side to finalize this divorce. The going rate for the dissolution was about $400. Hell, I offered to pay for it. It was a simple fix to me, but there was always an excuse. The red flags kept coming, as more and more issues came out of the woodwork—some of which were preventable, and some beyond his control. It was easy to overlook these things when my head was not clear.

I was truly envious of him. I wanted to be content with my life. How much peace I would feel if I was. I could not ever seem to get our values to align. Have I said I have a type? I know how to pick them? Strike 3. I had zero desire to settle for my life. That is something I refused to do, especially after my sister's passing. For me, trying to settle for my life when I was only making about $30,000 a year? Yeah, that wasn't going to work.

I appreciate him being there for me. This was the first person I would ever been with that generally wanted to make me happy. Hell, I did not know how to make me happy. But all good things must come to an end.

This time, I was starting over with experience. I moved out of my apartment, left everything, and moved back to Chari's home, where it all had started. I was back to square one. It is time to get my head on straight. It is time to focus and level up.

You have to make more income. You have to set yourself up to get a seat at the table. You owe it to yourself. Straighten your crown and get your head in the game. You are getting distracted again.

I was not ready for the beep beep—yes, you guessed it, another Mack truck was about to run my ass over.

# Chapter Eight

# **Who You Date**

I was glad my head returned. I was glad to remember my goals and ambitions. Now I had to get that thing on straight. Starting over from experience is very different from starting over from scratch. I had clear guidelines of what my next chapters were going to be.

I was job searching, looking to advance further in the food industry. Most of my experience was solely from working within that industry and customer service based. I could turn on the charm like no other. It did not matter that I had a horrible day; when I stepped into my role, I held my head high and I shined like I was supposed to. I may have been rolling burritos, but I took pride in every job I did.

There was not a job that was beneath me. I came from nothing. Anything forward was a step in the right direction. Forgiving, forgetting, and keeping your connections intact is important. I was not aware of this at the time, but I left all the companies I had worked at on good terms. I never wanted to burn bridges. if I had to do some resignations over, I would gladly do them differently.

When you are destined for greatness, and your life isn't aligning. You have to demand more from the universe. I did not want to be the worker bee for the rest of my life; no shade to any worker bees who constantly do it. Your goals are simply different from mine.

When you put out what you want and shift your mindset for the better, you will see opportunities everywhere. Stop looking at the bad and look for the good. The universe works in this way. You purchase a blue Toyota; you are in love with it. It's everything you wanted it to be. Suddenly, you start to notice so many blue Toyotas on the road.

The Law of Attraction is a philosophy that suggests that positive thoughts bring positive results into a person's life. I am the physical living proof of this. When you start looking at things positively, you start only to see the opportunities. Keeping your head in this mindset is a skill you must learn. It is hard to get you on that track, but when you master it, it's game over. This was the turning point in my life. This was where I learn the Law of Attraction. It was a bumpy start, but I got it down pat.

Moving into this newfound chapter of my life, I cannot say it was perfect. I was done dating. In the great words of RuPaul, "If you can't love yourself, how in the hell are you gonna love somebody else?" I was not concerned with loving someone else but focused on success and myself. I stopped looking. I was ready to take on the world. No more distractions, full speed ahead.

The moment that I did that, I was blindsided with a too-familiar Mack truck. Bryan had slid into my DMs after a three-and-a-half-year separation. I had mentioned I needed a new car on Facebook. Bryan reached out to me to test drive a car. I was in the market, but I could never afford a BMW. I decided to go to BMW in Dayton anyways. I told my ex that I was going. I was entirely upfront about who Bryan was, upfront that I was going to test drive a car. I was still engaged; I had nothing to lie about. Transparency is so important. I was not aware of how things would drastically change forever.

The man who raised me had recently passed, a few days before Thanksgiving of 2012. He was the closest thing to a dad. Tragedy had followed me losing my sister the year prior and then losing my dad the following year; we experienced so much loss. When losing a parent that never really seemed like one is weird. Its like they are gone. You look around and other people are devasted by this. Then you look at yourself. Lossing the man that help shape me was sad. Very sad. My bio father too passed several years later. All of my friends called me who had seen the news. Asking me how I felt. I replied "it's not a loss, I lost them years ago." You feel you should have felt something. When one person can cause you that much pain. It's easy to not feel loss. It was years later through extensive therapy that I was able to let go of the hate and bitterness. We can now call them dad instead of the sperm donor. You forgive them for yourself not them. I still tried to keep a positive outlook. I had been dead inside for years. Nothing had ever felt right. Nothing seemed to stick or fit or feel any sense of normal. I guess I felt like damaged goods.

I was thinking all of this while heading to the dealership, that driving a fancy BMW and catching up with Bryan might be a nice distraction. Even though I could never afford one, I still saw myself in a nice car. Never lose sight of those dreams, they will come in handy. The drive was long, about fifty minutes one way. I parked my little Fiat 500 out front. I headed for the showroom.

Bryan and I had not seen each other in over three years—heck we had not even spoken other than when he sent his condolences when my sister passed. I felt no emotion toward him. I opened the showroom doors on that big building, and holy cow, there he was, just as handsome as ever. Looking like a fine wine. It was like a jolt of electricity through my body. I remember thinking to myself, What the hell was that?

Honestly, I had not thought of Bryan since he broke my heart and smashed it into a billion pieces. Why would I? Unfortunately, he only came to mind when my ex proposed; Bryan was the first person that popped into my head. I thought it was a coincidence, even though I did not believe in them. Me being in mourning clouded my judgment. I never put much thought into it after that.

Emotions flooded me, like waves of electricity flowing through my body. I could not control them. In an instant, my thoughts returned to me. Like how I when my sister lived with us. Like how he was everything I ever wanted. Like the last time I felt safe. He was the last time I felt something real, something beyond me. Something bigger than both of us.

It's wild how one simple moment can bring you back to emotions you buried deep inside of you. Those emotions put you right back where you left off all those years ago. In that split second, I had no fear, no problems, and no pain. All was right in this single moment.

Bryan was with someone, and so was I. He had moved on from me, and I from him. We test-drove a car. It was A BMW X3. I thought to myself, I'll buy a car like this one day.

Bryan was the perfect gentleman; we had both been cheated on by multiple people and he knew my stance when it came to situations like this. He had recently found out my dad had passed; he gave his condolences for my dad and my sister. We talked for a little while, all in all, keeping it somewhat light.

The time came where I had to leave. Bryan asked if I had his number. I had deleted the number years ago. He had me add it to my phone. I told him we would have to go on a double date; I would bring my fiancé, and he would bring his date. He said with a chuckle, "You will never meet him."

At the time I did not understand that. It wasn't until later, I found he had ended his relationship months prior. Apparently, we both were trying to find our way in this life's tangled mess.

Leaving the dealership, I started heading home. It was strange. I had changed. I had no idea what was happening to me; something had shifted. Was it for the good? Also, what the hell was it?

Knowing my relationship was dead in the water, I was at peace over the next several weeks. We had been having problems for a good six months before this revelation. We had lost ourselves, not one of us in particular; we faded apart, mostly by my doing. I had come out of mourning. Things were not what I thought they were. I loved him; I do not regret him coming into my life. I might not be sitting here today writing if he had not. I don't have any ill will; leaving this relationship was one of the hardest things I had to do. We had different paths to go down. Sometimes, you grow apart for no reason. It was not fair to him. I had been dead inside for so long that I felt it was normal. In lots of situations in my previous relationships, I was numb at times, none of their fault solely. I had buried myself so far from ever feeling love that I had no idea what it was anymore. I will never be able to thank him enough for all he did; he was just being himself. I am forever grateful for that.

For the next several weeks, I was completely closed off from my relationship. I kept my mindset straight, with my eye on the prize. That prize was to be successful while creating a name for myself. I was struggling to keep my head in the right direction; subconsciously, it was heading in a completely different direction. I was not sure what it was.

Bryan had reached out several times. We talked. It was lovely to someone who knew my sister and my dad. Someone who knew my struggles and understood them. I think this is where some of the admiration came into play.

Bryan showed little to no signs of interest other than liking all of my social media late at night. That was okay. I could be the friend he needed.

Somewhere in the blur, I found myself going to a restaurant to meet him. Still to this day I am not sure how this happened. It legit just did. It was like second nature; it was so strange, almost like an energy field pulling at me. I was trying to figure out what was happening. Bryan and I had breakfast, again, some small talk.

Bryan has a law enforcement and military background. It was not hard for him to pick up on my unhappiness. He baited me. He got me to talk about how things had started to fall. How I was in mourning, how I did not have a clear mindset. I said I was unhappy, I felt this was unfair to my ex.

I can remember this like yesterday. He said, "Got it."

I was like, "Huh?"

He said, "I respected your relationship up to this point because that is what you deserve, and I know how you value it; however, the second I found out you were unhappy, there is no going back. You don't deserve to be unhappy. I will do everything in my power to make you happy."

Um. Whoa! The jolt was there again; I tried to push it down and hide it. I was so nervous I had no idea this was coming at me at the speed it was. Bryan leaned over and kissed me. HOLY HELL, when I tell you my body lit up like the Fourth of July, I mean it. My god, what was happening to me? It's like he had sent 1,000 volts of electricity through my body. I had to be glowing. What was happening? Everything faded away, and for the first time in so many lonely, hidden, numb days, it hit me. I was head over heels in love with this man.

In one instant, again, my entire life changed. There was no stopping the transfer of electricity between us. We did not even have to touch. He looked at me and smiled; he knew and felt it, too. He had never stopped loving me, and I had never stopped loving him. People ask me all the time, "How did you know?" It is simple: when you know, you just know. He is my best friend; he is my world. Some people search their entire life to find the kind of love we have, and they never find it. Fast forward eleven years later. We have been married for nine years. Bryan has built multiple divisions onto our cleaning business and it is busier and more successful than ever. When I tell you to trust your gut and take the leap. Do it. It will always be worth it.

When you look at successful people, look at who they align themselves with. People will tell you that you are too picky. Good. They'll say, "You aren't ever going to find someone with those standards."

Good. Set those standards high. One day you can tell them, "I can provide what I require."

Read that again and yell it louder for the people in the back. Never lower your standards to obtain what you want. You will make it happen. You're damn straight I'm picky; you have to pick the right person to grow with. Who you date can make or break you. If they are not helping row that boat, take another look. They might just be drilling holes to sink you.

Another secret to success is building with someone. If their goals match and challenge yours, get ready. you are about to take off. I say this all the time. Me alone, I am a badass. Us together, we are unstoppable. A force to be reckoned with. You must find the one who lights your world on fire, and in turn they fan your flames to make you shine that much brighter. Never settle for a personal or business relationship; you must know when to turn away or position yourself to shine brighter.

# Chapter Nine

# All in Good Time

The Law of Attraction is such a powerful tool. Demanding what you want will be one of the biggest, and most beneficial tools you can provide to yourself. I can remember how badly I wanted something; the answer was always "all in good time." Yes, having patience is a good thing.

Disciplining my work ethic throughout the years was hard. I kept punching the time clock daily, wondering if this is the best it will ever be. I kept looking at the notes I had written down of the things I wanted. I was being kinder to myself; I was talking to myself. Yes, it sounds weird, but it changes things. You start by hyping yourself up. When you get to the finish line for even the smallest of milestones, clap for yourself. Hang on to the feelings of achievement. You never know when you need to look back and see all of them.

I was goal-driven, working for a new company; I had a new environment, a new partner, and my friends. The grounds for success were laid, and I had an open runway. This was the year I broke free from it all. In that year, I said to myself that I will see myself as textbook successful. I will finally win. I would say these things to myself over and over, many times.

I loved working for the bagel company. Upper management appreciated my hard work. They liked my keen eye and attention to detail. I was among some of the first managers to pass a health inspection with flying colors. Most of their previous inspections failed or came close. I can remember moving out a fridge that was on wheels. Under the fridge was a pool of black mold water that had been there for years. It was gross. You should always work in clean environments. It puts you in a clear mindset. It can make your productivity much better.

I will never be the "go with the flow" type of guy. I always ask why. It is such a simple word that so many people are afraid to use. The next time you don't understand something, ask why.

There were instances at this place when this was needed. For example, you have to take the fiberglass cutting boards off the sandwich stations at night and place them in the walk-in fridge. Like huh? I asked why. You would have thought I asked the most difficult question they had ever heard. No one, and I mean no one, in the building knew why we did this every night. I asked them why again. Their response was, "That's how we have always done it."

How do you do a task every night and not know the reason why? That answer didn't work for me.

It was time to dig through the dreaded archives of books and manuals for this company. I finally found the answer. The boards were put into the walk-in fridge at night "to slow the growth of bacteria."

WTF, no way! Yes this was in the company manual.

I then grabbed both of those cutting boards and threw them in the dumpster. I ordered new plastic ones within the hour. I was told, "You can't do that."

Again, I asked "Why" and got no response.

Who knew how old those cutting boards were. If they were accumulating bacteria, and we are expected to slow the growth of bacteria, it was clearly time for them to go. In turn, eliminating these minuscule tasks sped up closing and helped overall cleanliness of the store.

Hear me out: Always ask why!

The bagel company had a fast-paced working environment, which I liked. I hate staring at the clock. I like to throw myself into my work and look up when it's time to go. I have never been one to stand around or milk a time clock. I could be doing a million other things than running out a time clock.

I started to mature in my managerial role. I had been in management for years at this point. This was another steppingstone to achieve my goals and pursue my dreams. I was in my early twenties—I think I was twenty-three or twenty-four. I earned the respect of my coworkers. I believe if you want respect, you must earn it. How will anyone listen to you if they have no respect for you?

I was never afraid of getting my hands dirty. If they needed help, I jumped in and helped. We were all on the same team and has the same goal; the operations paperwork could wait.

I started to understand that it was not about the number of hours you put in, it was about the quality of work you accomplished within those hours. The farther you move up the corporate ladder into management, the truer this becomes. Productivity plays a much bigger role than most people realize.

I was borderline stuck between worker bee and management. I had found this job due to the connections I had made, earlier when I said do not burn bridges and always do what is right, because someday you might have to stroll back across that bridge? While working at the burrito joint, my previous manager from the sandwich joint strolled in. Running into him was nice and weird at the same time. My old job was on the other side of the city. Why would he be here? He had not been able to save my job because he had been on paternity leave; he told me it was his regret and that what they did was not right or fair. He also ended up leaving his job, and taking a job at the bagel company. He asked me if I was interested in a position he needed to fill. I was shocked.

He said, "You were always on time and ready to work. You never called off, and your customer service is out of this world."

This was the first time my work ethic had ever been complimented. It was refreshing. I had been job hunting, so I contacted him for more details. He explained that I would need to work part-time at a different location until he was ready to transfer me to the busier store. I accepted the challenge. There was a pretty good pay jump. I had a proven track record and my wages reflected that.

I was offered the job without interviewing. Some other employees did not find this fair. I explained to them that I had always been a hard worker, had great references, and accomplished a lot, even considering my age. I took pride in every job I worked, which showed. Some understood why I had been hired in only a few weeks, and others were extremely intimidated.

I worked six days a week for two months at both jobs; sometimes, you play the long game to get where you need to go. Three weeks later, I took the supervisor position at the bagel company. It had been several years since I had worked with my previous manager, and we were different people now. It was refreshing that the tables had turned for me. Look how many doors opened when I got my mindset right and started using the Law of Attraction.

The company had a very diverse team, with many different kinds of people from different walks of life. It was great to work with people of different races and ages. Typically, when you visit restaurants in the fast-casual world, they employ the youngest and prettiest people. But if you can work and give it your all, you should be allowed to do so. I do not care if you are old, slow, or weird; everyone has a purpose and should be considered without prejudice.

Even though some of my coworkers were older than me, I earned their respect. I valued them. Getting people to do what I needed professionally was never hard. I would speak to them like human beings. Like someone's daughter, someone's mother, someone's sister. I think this gets lost in the busy hustle and bustle of the working class in America. We are all so consumed in working that we forget to be kind. I would never want someone to speak at me or yell, so why would I do that to anyone? It is a bagel, for Christ's sake; it is not that deep. No one died because their sandwich was made wrong or we did not have the specific bagel they wanted. No one died because they did not get their bagel fast enough. People are human; we make mistakes.

My career was blossoming. Everything seemed to work out for the better. I was recently engaged to the man of my dreams, and the bills were paid. Ah, finally, some peace.

The next several months seemed to be zip right on by. Working under the GM was like old times; we picked up right where we left off. Some new faces were hired, and they seemed decent enough, though I did not get a warm fuzzy feeling from them. They were forced hires by the assistant manager, who did not care too much for me. She seemed harmless enough. She had a very inflated sense of ego. She had been a training manager at the sandwich joint, before she came to work here. She would brag about her business degree. Her nose was permanently stuck in the air. her character was off. She was a scorned woman. A real man-hater. As much as I tried to get on her level, there was a constant divide. We did not mesh. I assumed it was jealousy, considering the circumstances in which I was hired. Any how I paid her no mind. My mind games could be just as good if not better than hers. She was the manager people could not stand.

Customers concluded she was two faced as they come. She was constantly contradicting herself. Customers would always have something negative to say about her.

Her joke of a managerial style was simple: yell, belittle, and bully her staff into submission. Her voice and breath would go wafting through the store; the odor and condescending verbiage of poorly educated words would shift the energy in the room so heavily. She did not care if customers were present when she was on a rampage. Everyone hated her. She was such a bitter person.

She had a business degree, but I am unsure where her education came from because business 101 is learning to talk to people. People are your biggest assets and biggest resources. I had finally met someone who was so far gone that there was zero reasoning with her. She was a narcissist. You cannot win against those individuals.

I started paying much closer attention to her. She was slowly removing the people she disliked, especially if they did not get on board with her condescending behavior. Mostly the ones she could not control. She would make up a crazy lie and run with it. She was a wrecking ball, and we could not get out of the way fast enough.

I will never forget I brought one of my friends and previous team members with me from my last job. My friend was making coffee and it spilled down the front of her, scalding her. When my friend went to clean the coffee off of her, that manager looked her in the face and said, "If you step off the line, you are fired."

Like what? Did she really just say that out loud?

After that she started gunning for my friend. Unfortunately, on a day when seven inches of snow fell, my friend chose not to risk her life and called off work because of the weather. She was fired for it. I think that manager was gunning for her so hard because she was friends with me. She was trying to cut off anyone who would side with me.

The next few weeks started to get interesting, watching

relationships form and alliances get made. The GM announced that he was leaving the company; he would have an acting GM and assistant to the GM until they could fill the position. This became a turning point, I was more qualified than anyone she had hired.

She tried like hell to talk her people up. Let's face it: toddlers could do better work than the yahoos she hired. She hired them because she could control them, like beaten dogs that were just thankful they had a place to call home. They had much lower IQs; that is how she operated. Anyone with half a brain would not follow her. She had them drinking the Kool-Aid.

Things started getting bumpy when people refused to come in to help cover call-offs; they would ask me if I was running the shift or if she was. Out of respect for her acting GM title, I would tell them it was her. They would then ask if she was staying the full shift, and would gladly come in if I said no. They knew if I was running the store things would flow better; they were okay coming in on their day off if she was not there.

When she called, they would never answer the phone. She would constantly say, "I don't know why everyone shows up for your shift but not mine."

I attempted to reason with her. I had several thoughtful conversations with her during which I simply said, "Yelling at people will never motivate them. I give respect and get it back in return."

I should have thought at this moment, is this lady intelligent enough to comprehend what I am saying? The answer was no. This would only fuel her hate fire. I was the last actual man standing in her way—at the least the only one with a set of balls that would call her out privately for her bullshit.

She couldn't stand me. I had everything she wanted: good title, respect for my coworkers, loving fiancé. It was the dream she had always wanted, and it was taken from her. I doubt she was the sole victim of her separation. It takes two to tango. I would try to level with her, coach and guide her, and get her to see we are all on the same team. The more I tried, the bigger the division. Her professionalism was nonexistent. If she liked you, she would talk to you about everything happening in the company, even entry-level coworkers. She would share information in personal files, people's pay, time off requests, and medical issues. Like a madman with a loaded gun in a crowd of people.

When she discovered my file, this was the atomic bomb; she lost her mind. She yelled, "How do you only make 100.00 dollars less than me?"

I was shocked; I had never had a manager question my wages publicly before. Trying to gather my thoughts like, Did this bitch just say that, I could no longer take the abuse. I felt like I was a kid again, making excuses for piss-poor behavior. I thought to myself, Someone needs to knock this bitch down a peg or two.

She yelled again. "I have a business degree, and you do not have an education."

Another dig, another character assassination. I could not believe she was doing this publicly.

I calmly turned around and said, "Oh, you only make that much more? I guess it is my resume and expertise in this field. You could have probably made more money if you had my demeanor."

Her face turned red. I thought she would explode. She looked like the Red Queen in Alice in Wonderland and even acted like her too. She thought I would back down in front of the employees; typically, due to my professionalism, I would have. Had she not loved hearing herself speak, she would have known that this calm and professional demeanor of mine was not made overnight. She thought she could bully me into submission. Think again. I took way worse beatings from people; she hadn't even scratched my surface. Do not mistake my kindness for weakness; you have no idea the kind of pain I had to endure to be this kind. The lion is not dead; he is sleeping.

# Chapter Ten

# The Ironic Guillotine

Some of the greatest inventors in history have met their demise in interesting ways. Google the story of who invented the guillotine; it's an ironic one.

Observation can be the best tool. An intelligent person does not speak in a room full of fools. The same could be said for me. That assistant manager was on a mission to get me out of the way.

When you observe and listen, I mean really listen, people will tell you precisely what they will do. Reading and studying people had become second nature to me. I was fascinated with people's thought processes. This tool came in handy. While she was on a path to take me down, I had been watching her.

She was sleeping with an employee. It was adorable, and she felt so superior that no one knew. I spotted it within weeks of my employment. Knowledge is power. Keep that ace in your pocket for a rainy day. She should have been watching her own back instead of readily trying to take everyone else down. Those closest to you will always do the most damage. They know your weaknesses and insecurities. Best believe they will use them to their advantage.

My fiancé had been in the military, and I would listen to how he structured things. How to get his point across without saying anything. I gained a lot of insight into how to control and defuse situations. I was taking in and locking all this information away. You never let them know how much you know. Remember, karma is a bitch, and she keeps receipts.

When you're living rent-free in someone's head, they become erratic and will do anything for people to look at you differently. Dulling someone else's shine will never make yours brighter. I had the support of all the employees and managers. The false and laughable accusations had to come first. Let's see, the first write-up I got was for, Oh, that is right, making gay slurs. Yes, you read that correctly: gay slurs. I guess I forgot that I was a gay man and was engaged to a man.

I argued that the lack of professionalism in the building was arguably the easiest way out of this. The manager that wrote me up had called me a flamer not even twenty minutes prior. The acting GM hated lesbians and used words like dyke, "those people." I guess this was acceptable when it came from the dictator-acting GM. Let me give her a name so this is not confusing. KAREN sounds about right. Karen could say whatever she wanted about all the other staff, but when a gay man does it, it is too much. Conveniently, the complaint was made by the employee who was sleeping with her.

My new title came through. I was promoted again with flying colors and praises. I was the assistant manager; Karen received the GM title by default. I was considered, and my name was tossed in the ring more than once. She had been there longer than me. Upper management was not sure she could handle it. She had been caught crying in the parking lot during lunch rush—poor thing.

During this time, I was not aware that I had kidney stones. We were out one night at a friend's home when it hit me like a ton of bricks. I collapsed in the front yard and was rushed to the ER.

I was unable to make it to work. My fiancé had to call in

for me due to my being incapacitated. He even sent her my medical record and a picture of me dying in a hospital bed. I returned to work the next day. I had to work; I couldn't afford to take time off. I had bills to pay. Karen asked for my doctor's note. My doctor ordered me to be off work for five days. She felt the need to report me to HR. I was forced to take the PTO that I had so gallantly accumulated.

After my forced time off, I returned to work and was met with two write-ups, calling off incorrectly because my fiancé did it and only reporting to the manager on shift, which was policy. She wanted me to call her at her home, even if she was off for the day. She also said I should have called daily to reiterate my progress even though I was using my PTO.

She went on a manager meeting call one day with all the managers in the company and mocked me openly to everyone. I finally went over her head and reported her to the district manager. I asked for a transfer; I gave them all the correct information and how I took the proper channels. He said he would think about it.

I reported her again two weeks later. Again, he would think about it.

I went to multiple other locations to ask the managers for help or guide me through this. Any location would welcome me in with open arms. I had picked up shifts at all their stores to help out. When other stores needed staffing, we are all on the same team. Those managers were also met with "I will think about it."

The final straw came when the store was short-staffed again and the bagel oven had jammed again, a common issue within this store. Bagel ovens are enormous; you can stand inside them. Let me tell you, this bitch dead on the phone told me to climb into a hot oven to retrieve bagels that were inside and going to burn. She wanted her bonus and didn't want food costs to be too high, although at the end of the day, the bagels were tossed in the trash, and chemicals were poured over them so people experiencing homelessness wouldn't get them. It was super dangerous.

I told her, "I will not be climbing in the oven."

All of the policy handbooks said never to do this. The next day, I was met with my final write-up: if there were any following incidents, I would be terminated from the company.

I could not believe she had the audacity to write me up for burnt bagels. Something clearly beyond my control. That was it. She had won the battle. I looked dead in her face. "You will never get the satisfaction of terminating me. I will have my two weeks' notice turned in this evening."

You must move stealthily through the night and never be backlit. Bryan taught me that. I was feeding them lies, because ole messy face (KAREN) was busy listening to her spies. She never saw it coming. You know, she was playing checkers, I was playing chess.

*Chapter Eleven*

# Checkmate, Bitch

The next several weeks, she gunned for me. My working reputation had never been tarnished. I had multiple letters of recommendation written for me over the course of my career, most of which were from my previous managers, offered to me when I put in my resignation.

These were consistent reminders for me to stay true to myself. They consisted of thank you letters and how valuable of an asset I was. Generally, my managers thanked me for always being kind and understanding.

When you receive these, a lot of the noise gets focused out; you understand that your purpose here is not to be successful. Your purpose is much more significant. My purpose was to help people. I know this now. Whether I am in people's lives for a few moments or multiple seasons, I would only like to be remembered for being kind and showing up. I hope people will say that I was always helping anyone in need that I could.

When you have been hurt, you learn always to protect yourself. Oh, you know me and that damn wall. Anyway, it is the quiet ones you must watch out for. They are constantly listening and taking in all the information. I learned through a leadership book that you should always document everything, even if it is irrelevant. I've been blessed with somewhat of a photographic memory. I take it all in and analyze it. It is a trauma response, I know; I am working on it.

The last two weeks were crucial. Karen underestimated me again. She thought I was not aware that if you do not work your full two weeks' notice of your scheduled shift, you forfeit all of your PTO Your employment status would be considered terminated, not voluntarily departing the company.

It became a game for me. She would demand something that needed to be fixed quickly, which would be detrimental to the company's smooth operation. I would wait or finish up with a customer and come to her side. She needed me. I was a key component to the smooth operation of the shifts; a bruised ego blinded her that she missed it.

Again, I'd look at my watch. "Oh, look at the time. One minute passed. I am off."

Who knew how much one minute could mean? Who knew the relevance of the one-minute-late write-up that held so much power?

The last day had finally come. I was about an hour from my scheduled time out. The store was incredibly understaffed again; this had grown into the business's normal operations. She ran everyone off that was good. She could not keep anyone to save her life. I guess that is how it goes.

Suddenly, her timid lap dog emerged. The coward could not even look me in the eyes, man to man. He said, "Something came up and you need to stay over three hours."

I laughed. I looked at him, thinking he was joking. He was staring at the floor. I said, "I am off at 10am; I am leaving at 10am.

He again said, "But Karen said you have to," in a wimpy baby voice.

I again turned to him with cold, dead eyes. "Are you, my

boss? Are we going down this road again?"

Knowing damn well I could fire his ass on principle, he quickly and cowardly scurried away.

Another half hour went by, and he hid in the back, overwhelmed with the influx of customers and his emotions. I was seamlessly handling the volume. I may be a bit hood at heart, but my customer service voice went to Harvard.

Again, he emerged. Instead of helping his team, he started pacing. He approached another employee who had respected me from day one and told her the same thing.

She said, "No, I am off at 10am. I am leaving at 10 am."

My, how the mighty had fallen. He had enough staff on his side that if he had too, he could run the shift fine. However, that would require hard work, and he was not going to break one single bead of sweat. He was, as she had told him, "the manager when I leave, and he doesn't have to do that."

See, that is the thing about ego. It can be your death. You always must be aware of people's egos.

He approached me and handed me the store phone, which had been ringing for about 45 minutes, while he was pacing, and while we were all working. I take the phone while making sandwiches with a line out the door. I recognized the voice like nails on a chalkboard. Karen. She was oddly a bit emotional.

She explained that her relative was in the hospital, which unfortunately was not a big surprise. He had been sick. She again demanded I stay for only three more hours, putting me on a twelve-hour shift.

When I came in at 2am, I was forced to work the shift I wasn't hired for. In my employment file, I was hired and told I would be working the 7am-3pm shift. She had a copy of it. I was forced into this shift three months prior. My character was still intact. I said, "I am very sorry to hear about your relative being in the hospital; I will stay..."

You could tell she felt relief; her lap dog, listening in, sighed in relief.

To finish my statement, I said, "I will stay... Only One Minute past my scheduled time out. Goodbye."

I headed for the back door and the sad little lap dog was there. He looked at me. I grinned and said, "This is your problem now, Manager. You wanted my job so bad, so have fun."

I tossed my building keys at him, hitting him in the chest, and walked out the door with my two other employees in tow. I yelled as loudly as I could, "I'm FREE!"

Upon your voluntary departure from the company, the protocol is an exit survey. Only a few people get these; most of the time, the upper management drives you to your breaking point, so you leave and lose your leverage in the company. Not me; I followed all the rules to a tee. I had all the policies copied when I was not on shift.

She felt she was so clever because she had won the battle. However, I won the war. Luckily for me, I had spies, too. I was documenting everything for about a month or so before my exit. I had dates, time stamps, and all the communication on every shift on which she was present. I named all the employees who were present with their emails and phone numbers; I also tossed in their employee badge numbers for extra measure.

I added and named every manager on the call when she publicly blasted me for the weather. The managers gladly took my side. I added the recordings of her name-calling. Her minions, whom she thought she had in her corner, sent me everything I needed from the days I was not on shift. When she thought no one was watching. I added the other managers at the other stores; they were quickly released from their positions.

The funny thing about Facebook is that you can

find people easily when you did not have access to them originally. Coincidently, all the managers who were forced to leave their stores happened to be LGBTQ. Now, this was before the Supreme Court overturned the marriage ban on gay couples. We had zero protection from being terminated for being gay. I have never had to use that card until it was not just me being hurt. It was others. They all were currently lawyering up. Her harassing employees recorded evidence; you name it, I had it. I lost count of how many pages of documentation I had on her and her puppets.

My exit survey finally came in. I meticulously filled out every inch of those text boxes. I was not sure if it would matter. I planned to copy all the pages and put them together like a manuscript, which is pretty fitting now while I write one. I didn't know if it would make a difference if anyone would listen.

I took my first vacation when I was twenty-four years old. I had only experienced one short vacation when we were young. My mom had scrounged up every penny we had to drive us to Florida when I was fifteen.

While vacationing and walking on the beach, weirdly my phone rang. It was the corporate headquarters of the bagel company, and they wanted to know if I had time to talk to them. I was obliged; I was put on speaker phone in a conference room full of the decision makers. You you could hear a pin drop as I told the story.

I would not know the outcome of this phone call I for a few months. I had to call in on several occasions to get my PTO released. I put in so many hours that I had accumulated about three weeks of PTO. I needed the payout. This job had done me in. My hard work, my loyalty, was for nothing. Another job on the resume. It hit me in the feels. It took me out at the knees. I vowed never to work in food again.

A week went by and I received a phone call from them. If I returned, I would be offered an additional $10,000- raise. I again said, "No. For me, it's the principle."

I needed the job desperately, but you must stay true to your core. I had felt so much peace with my decision. No one would make them for me anymore.

A day or two went by, and I got another phone call, only this time it is a friend of mine. She was an OG manager at another location.

She said, "Holy shit, what the hell did you do?"

That reaction took me aback. I had no clue what she was referring to. I said, "I have no idea what you are talking about."

She said, "Well, apparently, you cleaned house." Which is now ironic, since I clean houses for a living.

I replied, "I'm still lost about what is going on."

She went on to say, "Corporate sent out new policies, and things are rapidly changing. The district manager was fired, the manager that originally hired you was fired, another store manager was fired." (The buddy of the dreadful Karen). "Oh, and the best part of all, Karen has been fired!"

I am not going to lie. I thought I was dreaming.

Do not ever underestimate the power of knowledge. It will come in handy in many ways throughout your life. Sometimes, things do not work out because better things are to come. Another crazy full-circle moment to come out of this. It seems false, but this happens when you demand what you want. Good things come to those who wait.

My friend, Elaine, who had been burnt by the coffee maker—the one Karen told she'd be fired if she left the line—called me several years later. Elaine now works for a huge accounting firm. She decided she wanted to get some Starbucks on her lunch break. She ordered her normal cup of coffee and went to the end of the counter to pick it up. When she looked up, you'll never believe who had made her coffee for her. It was KAREN! How is that for some karma? Checkmate, bitch!

*Chapter Twelve*

# The Side Hustle

This is where things get fun.

After the bagel company, I worked odd jobs here and there and did not want to be another number who worked for a corporation. I am Trenton, I am destined to do epic shit! I deserve a seat at the table. What would I do to sit at that table? Do you know how much I can bring to that table? What did I want to do?

Bryan suggested that I clean houses. I had always done this as a bit of side hustle. When friends of mine moved in and out of places, I offered to help with the cleaning for a bottle of wine. Could this be something?

I love to clean. It calms me down. It helps me think. It is constantly changing, and it is always something different. But I doubted myself. I thought things like, People like me cannot do that. Things like this do not happen to people like me. Then I told myself, There you are again, second-guessing yourself, thinking you cannot. Demand it; good things come to those who wait. Then I reasoned: Well, we desperately need the money. I guess it cannot hurt to give it a try. At least cleaning houses will get me by for the time being.

How this course of action would slowly turn into something. . .

When you sit down and truly listen to what you think, what you feel, listen to your gut, you start to realize: All my knowledge and experience had to count for something. I wanted a seat at the table and I had waited long enough.

I got tired of waiting. I built my own damn table! That's right, let's get going.

I do not think I would change any of the crazy things that have happened to me. They have made me the man I am today. Struggles make you stronger, wiser, and humble.

When I started Trenton's Helping Hands LLC, it was me, a mop, and a Fiat. I did think I would only do this temporarily to make ends meet. I made my own hours, which is what I wanted. I could take out the middleman and pay myself what I felt I deserved.

Could this work? Could this be something someday?

Well, I can tell you. It is something. After hitting a few minor bumps, I got focused and start building my dreams. My dream of making it. My dream of being successful. Success is not defined by anyone but you. After making so much money, I thought I was successful. I could be like, "Dang, I am rich." But you are never truly wealthy until you have something money cannot buy: Freedom. Free from it all. I have often been asked what I want out of life. Is it fancy cars? Homes? Yachts? My answer has always remained the same.

"Why did you build this company?" my team members have asked me over the years. "What do you want?"

I want my time. I started this company so I could have my time back. My life is back. We waste so much time on nonsense. The harsh reality is none of us is leaving here alive. This is no dress rehearsal; we do not get do-overs. So what are you waiting for? Your time is now. Demand it!

The biggest lesson I have learned is learning your niche. What are you good at? How can you perfect that and repeat it perfectly? Every single time. It is all about consistency.

I wish I could lead you to a magic pathway that will give you everything you have ever wanted, but we don't live in a world where false realities exist. How did I get here?

While my friends were partying in their early twenties, I cleaned houses. I know cleaning houses is not the most glamorous job in the world. People looked down on me all the time. Some of the clients I used to clean for talked down to me because I was a house cleaner.

People want you to do what they think is right. What they have been taught. What they think is normal. Guess what? They are not you. I took a different path. I threw myself into the cleaning world, feet first. You will never know if you do not try. The answer is always no if you do not ask.

I kept on cleaning. I put in those hours again, only this time, I was not slaving away for someone else; I was slaving away for me. This made it so much easier to put in the hours. My time was now.

I would get tired, but I kept on cleaning. I was slowly tossing my name into the ring to find clients. I went door to door with flyers, hanging them up in subdivisions, never getting any phone calls. I get calls now from people I once worked for.

Keeping those connections open, holding to my core, and never straying from my mission—this has helped me so much along the way. Your life is what you make of it. I could have become a product of my environment and played victim. I never let that define me; I let it thrive me. I will say this to the day I die: If you want it bad enough, you will find a way; you will not make excuses.

For years, I would go to neighborhoods and hang up doorknockers, getting very little response in return. But then you get that one client. That client whose job you pour your heart and soul into. Then that client helps open doors for you.

I just kept cleaning houses. I kept showing up. Reliability

is half the battle; your consistency will put you far ahead of the competition.

You would be alarmed to know how many businesses open for a few months, then go under. The amount of business I have seen come and go is alarming. Statically speaking, 20 percent of new businesses fail during the first two years of being open, 45 percent during the first five years, and 65 percent during the first ten years. Only 25 percent of new businesses make it fifteen years or more.

Do not let these numbers scare you. Your business will be what you put into it. I never thought I would be considered an entrepreneur. When you are first starting, you wear all the hats. All the titles. I found this to be a huge advantage. I started this business in my garage. I had a mop and a Fiat, remember? The little side hustle that turned the tables for me.

You do not have to reinvent the wheel to make it happen. Find your niche and make it better than anyone else. That will get you started on the right path. Remember the table you are building. Your brand, your experiences, it is all relevant.

Block out the naysayers. Move in silence. Most people will to try to help and guide you. They will try to talk you out of it. Tell you to give up. You will eventually start second-guessing yourself. Those are not your people. Never take business advice from someone who has no idea what they are talking about. You will never be criticized by someone who is doing more than you.

A side hustle can be just that—something you do on the side. It can also be the start of achieving big dreams.

A have a client who has become one of my closest friends. I was doubting myself. I struggled. All my friends had formal educations and "real" jobs. I said to this friend, Nicole, "I don't have a real job like some people do."

She said back to me, and these words rang so true for

me then and still to this day do, "You may not have jobs like them, but dude, you own a business."

That connection came from the one and only time I had ever advertised my business on Craigslist. Had I not let my pride down and gotten on Craigslist, I would not have made this connection, this friend.

She wanted me to win. She did not know that she was what I needed at that moment. She had no clue how that was such a defining moment in my life: The first time I was able to see myself, a little poor hillbilly kid, as a business owner.

I returned the favor several years later when she was struggling. I was able to be the pillar she needed, and I was able to be the light in her darkness. She is now doing better than ever.

Sometimes everything falls apart so that you can rebuild. The things you thought were never possible start to become possible. You see how the littlest connections mold your place in the universe.

Get your support system, get the right people in your corner, and get your head in this game. I will not tell you this is easy. It is not. I have spent many years pouring my blood, sweat, and tears into this company, building this brand. You must be able to pour every bit of yourself into it. You must bleed for it. Then, bleed some more. Only then will you be able to push your dreams into reality.

# Chapter Thirteen

# How Big Are You Willing to Dream?

Some of the most successful people in the world started from nothing. There are many self-made millionaires.

When I started, I had zero financial backing, so I purchased chemicals right off the Family Dollar shelf. No shame in my game. You must start somewhere.

I did not anticipate that people would keep talking about me. I had maybe ten houses, and people kept talking about me. In a way, they were like my little brand ambassadors. How did I get them to do this? I provided them with a fair-priced service. I then perfected that service. I then repeated that perfected service meticulously and repeatedly. I could do it in my sleep until it was burnt into my brain.

My next several years were good. The ups make you appreciate the downs. When you are just starting, you do not have all the answers. You have an idea but not the answers. You will think that you can undercharge your time to win the bid. Or, you know the person and want to give them your services at a lower rate. This is one dangerous game. Unfortunately, I had to learn this the hard way twice.

The first time, I had no overhead, maybe a few hundred dollars in supplies and a car payment. Working a lot of hours, not making ends meet. I did a lot of research on why most businesses fail. There are several reasons. With insufficient funding or knowledge, the owner gets too big for their britches, gets ahead of themselves, opens too fast, and runs into cash flow problems. Another is that the owner is rapidly expanding; they take their eyes off it because they lose interest in doing the work. They end up cutting corners, usually with training, then their staff are not equipped to put out the fires. These kinds of things will kill your reputation faster than you can imagine. This industry is cutthroat; someone is always willing to undercut your numbers. They can come in swiftly and before you know it, your best client is gone.

Start slow. Your real timeline to get your company up off the ground, especially if it is built from scratch, will be around the third or even fourth year in business, if you can keep your consistency and performance in check.

I feel lucky that I had such terrible experiences leading up to the point where I wanted to build my table. I had all the best examples of the kind of business owner and leaders I never wanted to be. I can remember when I did not have any employees. I still made lists for them. I added policies before I even needed them. Why, might you ask? I wanted to make sure that I never ended up even remotely close to the bad managers I had known.

I read leadership books for no reason other than wanting to learn. When I found the right employee, I wanted to know that they would see I was not like everyone else and that I was not in this to make money. I wanted to build something that had not been built before. Something no one had seen. Something sustainable. A place where people wanted to work. Where they wanted to belong. Not because of the money but because of the core culture.

The culture in a company starts at the top. Leaders must educate themselves constantly. You must guide your people. You must build the dream company—not just where people want to work, but where people want to do business.

Creating lifelong connections and opening doors that would have never been built or even seen.

To understand what makes a business good, strip it all away. You must see the bones. When you strip it down, the foundation must be built correctly, not rushed. The culture will still be there. That is how you start growing and building that dream. When the bones are good, try to knock them down. Are they solid? If they are, then find all the weakest points. Get your plans together and sit down with someone you trust. Have them start negatively ripping your bones and foundation apart. Have your friends use a jackhammer and dig up every inch of it. Pull out all the nails, pull out all the screws, let them find the holes. Let them find the holes you fixed and write down all the negativity about your business.

Then find the next friend you trust and repeat this process. Allow that friend to shred your business. Then when that's done, pick up the phone and find another friend, yep, you guessed it, to run those bones over with a steam roller.

Record what they tell you or write it down on paper. Then return to your drawing board, desk, and dining room table, floor. Lay everything you have learned out in front of you. Sit with it for a few moments. Count to ten, looking at all the weak spots your friends so easily found.

Now, start over and reinforce the foundation of your business. Those weaknesses are right out in front of you. This will be better than getting into it and being blindsided by something so simple. When attempting to establish yourself in the building stages, being blindsided can be the difference between being in business or going under. This is a tool I wish someone used with me. It would have saved me money and time and significantly fewer headaches. You live, and you learn, but let these words stand true: The house does not fall when the bones are good.

Now, what is the next move? How big are you willing to dream? If your dreams do not scare you, they are not big enough. One of my most favorite sayings is, "If you think the cost of winning is too high, wait until you get the bill for regret."

*Chapter Fourteen*

# No, No, and No

Some of the biggest lessons I learned have been from being told "No" and "No thank you," and "Not today" or "I don't have the time, not interested." I couldn't count the number of nos I've gotten from people. The door slam is typically the hardest.

However, you learn from the door slams. You get to see all kinds of people. All different walks of life: Privileged, poor, educated, uneducated. All these classes have one thing in common: They are all still human.

When I overcame a goal that I worked tirelessly to achieve, I immediately say to myself, Wow, look how far I have come. It was not easy. It was extremely challenging. Building your dreams will keep you on the right track. Just stay focused.

Achieving goals changes you, but I always try to remain humble. It has given me more insight than the many lessons I have learned. This is an important key when you come from humble beginnings. It radiates something in you that most people see, and you sometimes do not even see yourself.

My clients have wanted me to win; they have believed in me. Heck, probably before I believed in myself. Some connections work out for the better, and even the connections that don't are still connections.

I remember getting a message from a new client who needed some help around the house. I was thrilled as this was my eighth house. She explained where she lived, and I was aware of the road; I had traveled it many times to go to the grocery store.

I was so excited to have a client near where I grew up. You get one chance to make a good first impression. My friends would always tease me. I would always have a shaved face and put on my nicer clothes. I always wanted to present myself in a manner of respect. Especially for their time. I promise that showing up fifteen minutes early and being presentable is half the battle.

I had almost made it to the address and thought there was no way that was the house she had called me about. The home was stunningly, beautifully built. It was picturesque, with so much charm. It sat at the end of a long paved driveway, lined with a few small trees . The landscaping was impeccable. It was something out of the story books.

This house was so  vivid in my head from when I was a kid. We would pass by these homes on the way back to our less-desirable trailer. I always wished to just once to see the inside of that house.

This was the full circle moment, the humbled moment. I was right where I needed to be.

The client took me on. I was so thankful. She became one of my longest-standing and most loyal clients in my ten years so far in business. She stood by me through thick and thin. She wanted me to win. These clients are one and a million. When you find them, take care of them. You may not even be aware that they became some of your biggest supporters.

The cleaning industry is hard. There is always someone willing to do it cheaper. They can almost always undercut your number. However, when those people come knocking, my clients do not entertain them.

I have delivered a superior service through all the ups and downs. I sometimes have had to clean a home alone when another employee decided not to show up, but I had to keep pushing forward. The show must go on. Just because I did not have the staff did not mean I would cancel. I pushed through. It was a large home. It would kick my butt, but while I was there cleaning, I remembered why I started. It would only fuel my desire to be successful.

Keep pushing through the hard times, and the good ones will come. Most people give up in the first or second year of business. I had put all my eggs in this basket, which had to work. I did not have my parents; I was not privileged enough to have a second option. There was no safety net, this had to work. Let that desire fuel you. Demand what you want from this universe.

Another significant moment for me came when I was trying to market myself. At that time, I was hanging up door knockers in a neighborhood where I thought I wanted to live. I am sure I had hung up about a hundred door knockers. Days turned into weeks, and there were no calls. I was used to not getting the calls. I do not know if I was in their shoes, I would have called either.

One afternoon, the phone rang. This client changed my entire perspective. She was the only one to call me back out of the whole area of Ross. She asked if I could come out and give her a quote. I gladly accepted.

This home was another impressive home. You can feel their warmth, love, and happiness when you step inside. I find it incredibly difficult to explain, but it was a bizarre feeling. She took me on with no questions asked. She was very impressed with my work. Considering my age, I think she felt that I would come once and not show up again. However, I did; I showed up every month right on time, not knowing the importance of it.

She told me years later she would run her husband out of the home so he would not be in my way. She was warm.

Kind. Loving. She was the only one out of those hundreds of door knockers hung who believed in me. I could barely afford the fifty dollars it had cost me to get them printed, and she changed all of it for me.

I really started to see the potential in myself. I started looking at ways to sharpen my skills. Thankfully, design school taught me all of the correct names of items in homes. I could decide on the different types of stone for counters and backsplashes. People seemed to like that I knew these types of things. I could tell you the difference between a baluster and spindle. Some useless knowledge for some, but not for me. I soaked up all the information I could about home cleanliness.

Some people treat you differently when you tell them you clean homes. Their response often is, "How hard can it be. It is just cleaning houses. It is just pushing a sweeper around."

Many people have no idea what it takes to finish three to four homes a day, with little or no errors. I found out how to get stainless steel to buff in without smears. I learned the difference between oil-based and water-based stainless-steel cleaners. I kept pushing forward, learning to shove everyone out of the way who doubted and put me down. I can still remember sitting at a table of people when I told them I cleaned houses for a living. They thought I had nothing to offer to the conversation. They laughed at me in year one; I am now laughing at them at year ten.

I started gaining a lot of traction when it came to new clients. This was when I learned that my knowledge of this industry was worth something. Allowing people to tell you what they think your worth is should never fly. That becomes a dangerous game. I go the furthest extra mile for clients who have said, "I think that job was only worth $50, so that is what I am paying," or "What did you even do here? Did you even clean?"—knowing damn good and well, I put my heart and soul into that clean to impress them.

Another person not paying me.

Those clients will make you wise. They will make you appreciate the solid foundation you have made with your regular clients. Know your worth. Do not let anyone tell you differently. A house cleaner or a brain surgeon both have their worth.  If it doesn't feel right, TRUST me, walk away. You will never know how hard it is to try to make them happy.

Through all these new lessons, I always keep my regular clients happy. I always kept them on the front lines of importance. Your solid clients should always be the main priority. The last thing you want when you are expanding is to lose those anchor clients.

Still sometimes all your perfected work will fall short. You will lose loyal clients, and be unaware of the reason. One of my first clients went off schedule— the client who had been the only one who called me from that door knocker I had put out. I could not for the life of me figure out why. For months, I wondered if I had failed her. If I had been too busy and missed something or missed a sign.

I went on for months wondering if I could have done something different.

Remember when I said to keep those connections at all costs? I got a call back from her. She assured me she was traveling. I was so excited, I thought, Okay, thankfully she was not upset with me. I am going to get that second chance.

Even though I was cleaning for her daughter now. I still loved having her a part of the cycle of cleaning. I was telling my new crew about her; how they would enjoy her. Yes, she was sometimes, particular, but if you kept her happy, she ensured you have the hours.

I arrived at the house with my crew for the first cleaning in several months. I was extremely excited to start again. Seeing her after all this time she looked way different. She was now super tan.

I said, "Well, traveling looks so good on you."

She smiled softly and let us in.

I started the crew on the house and quickly realized that her other children were in town, which was an odd time of year for them to be there. Her husband was also at home. Again, strange, since she usually runs him off. The atmosphere in the home was bleak.

She approached me and said, "I did not get a great tan. I have stage 4 pancreatic cancer."

My heart sank. I was in disbelief. I could tell she was worried. I put on a stern face and didn't let her see the shock that overtook my whole body.

While cleaning, I couldn't help but overhear rumbles of conversation. Usually, I blocked out most of my client's conversations completely. Clients have a right to privacy. But these conversations were very hard to block. It was all I could do to put on a brave face to finish that cleaning.

When the cleaning was done, we said our goodbyes, knowing this would unfortunately be the last time I would get to see her.

I barely made it to the car; I just lost it. The tears seem to overcome me. My crew always looked at me as strong, typically holding my own and making it look easy. The loss that the family would feel would be devastating. I won't go further on this topic because I respect her and her family. They are still on my client list.

This is when you look back and remember what got you here. This is where you recognize that you were kind. You went out of your way to do the right things. You had their back. You also never know when you will not get the chance to say what you want.

I do have something I wish I would have said to her: "Thank you for believing in me. Thank you for pushing me. Thank you for the opportunity to believe in myself. I hope you know that by knowing you, you changed my life. I will forever be eternally grateful for you and your entire family." With all those no's, I am so glad she was that one yes.

*Chapter Fifteen*

# **Revise, Rebuild, Restructure**

Undoubtedly, there will come a time when you have bitten off way more than you can chew and you will ask yourself, "Why am I doing this?" and "I want to win, but at what cost?"

You will question every turn, every motive, and everything in between.

You crossed those lines and you wanted to succeed; you missed all the red flags and have dragged good employees with you. You are all burnt out, and you are tired.

Why? Was it me? Was it something I did? What am I doing wrong? I cannot ask them to keep doing this.

This is the fine line between business workers and business owners. When this time comes, you will struggle to get through it. More lessons are still to be learned.

Sure, when the business took off, you could jump around and wear all the hats. Then it became more straightforward with a team backing you. Your decisions affect the entire team and the entire company simultaneously. I wish there was an easy answer for this one. There isn't one. What makes sense to you might not make sense to the team.

This is where your leadership will start taking over. People will be looking up to you. You must guide and coach them. Your purpose is much bigger than ensuring the ship is being rowed evenly; you are now the one who must inspire your crew. You are the captain now, and you must navigate the ship. When you step into this role, you should almost immediately start furthering your education in leadership.

People are such complex beings. One word is the difference between smashing into the rocks out of nowhere, opening all the sails, and leaning the ship dangerously on its side to avoid the stones escaping the pirates. You will be influencing in rooms you never thought would be possible. You will look up one day for the answers, and everyone will be looking at you. Talk about a shock. Some are destined for leadership. I am a Leo and have always felt the need to go against the wind, take the path less traveled, and shake things up. We are the artists, the forces, the ambitious. You never know what you can do. You might be crazy enough to change this world.

This is where things get bumpy—when you realize the things that worked initially do not even come close to working now. In the beginning, you gave in, your team backed you, and you backed them. You would let the company take the backseat to some of your employees. You allowed such bad habits that it is too late to break them. Those bad habits are now rubbing off.

Toxicity should not be in the workplace. It is a cancer it eats the company from the inside. It takes down everything and everyone in its place. It is a bomb, slowly ticking till it decides to blow. That is how cancer starts.

This is when REVISE steps in. You go back through all of your processes to assess what do you need to change so this never happens again. Get out your highlighter; we have some work to do. You will be shocked at how many things no longer fit and how vague your processes are. It is time to revise them all, and I mean for ALL—owners are included in that too. You are the leader. You have to set an example of which way this ship is headed. The methodology is beautiful. It has its purpose, and that purpose is now.

You will no longer allow things to slide. You will be forced to set examples, even of some of your best workers. If you let one slide, they will all feel allowed to slide. Once you deeply understand this, check back in six months to a year. Business is constantly changing. You must change it.

We must rebuild the broken things, whether it is your teams, bank accounts, or technologies. We must rebuild the company from the ground up. What works and what does not? Trim the fat. If someone on your staff does not align with the core values, they cannot work for your company. They must go. Trim the fat quickly with no hesitation listen to your gut; it will be worth it in the end.

Let one person get away with this and they will hold your entire company back—it is time to let them go. I do not care if they are your biggest closer. If they cannot push your culture, this is not the place for them.

You need doers, not askers. You must let them fail. If they never do, they will never learn. You can guide them all day long, but if you keep them from hitting the floor, it teaches them nothing. You are wasting your time on another employee who is choosing not to perform. Did it occur to you no one is now driving the ship? Keep your eye on where it needs to be navigating.

These hard lessons will all be worth it in the end. Set them up to win. Your most prominent people will come to you and ask, "How do I fix this?"

This is an important lesson. You should respond like this. Say nothing and stare at them until they start using their brains. They will give you some examples to make them implement one. If it is the wrong decision, explain why, have them own it, and move on. Mistakes happen. Making no moves is failing. Making the wrong ones is learning.

Restructuring is the hardest of all. Is the company struggling? Then stop taking on more. It will not get better until you find the problem and restructure it. What is the problem? Is it your training? Is it your onboarding? Is it your price?

Now we are ready for the deep dive. If you have not done a deep dive into every aspect of this company, now is the time to do it. Do you think you have it all figured out because you've made it this far? Little hint: You do not have it figured out. I still learn something new every single day. As a business owner or entrepreneur, you will learn, grow, evolve. You will meet your mental capacity, and when things start getting hard, you will level up.

Revise, Rebuild, and Restructure until you are running a fine-oiled machine. Even then, you still want to revise every year. Then teach all this to your next in line or your biggest hitter who wants more.

I always build my team. My team consists of people with better skills set than me. You will not know everything. Learn from your team and they in turn will learn from you. if the team is made up of people with all different skill sets that align with each one of your departments. You are setting the road map to success. That is what makes us all change. Put a fresh pair of eyes on it. Sometimes we cannot see what's sitting right in front of us.

This will challenge the way you see the future. You constantly want to be challenged; if you are not, you are getting distracted again. You have multiple companies to run. If you want success, get up and make it happen. You owe it to yourself.

Then, look back and see how far you have come. Reflect on the good, the bad, and the freaking ugly that got you here. Try not to make those mistakes moving forward. You are finally starting to think like an entrepreneur. If your business is not growing, it is dying.

Be honest, be raw, and tell your team when you mess up. You should be brainstorming to not end up where you currently may be. There is nothing wrong with starting over. I have started over more times than I can count. It is the struggles that make you stronger. They get you ready to go to battle when you need to.

Remember, do not doubt yourself. You have got this far. Keep going. There is so much more life worth living. When we are young, we are programmed to think we cannot do it. We will not make it. I am here to tell you that if you try and you fail, congratulations. Ninety-two percent of people will not even try. Get back up and do it again. You have got dreams to build, not people to impress.

# Chapter Sixteen

# Manifest to the Extreme

I would have laughed at you if you had told me years ago that manifesting the life you want was a thing. We hear people say this all the time.

When I was younger, I dreamed of having a big home, a perfectly manicured lawn, beautiful timepieces, and luxury cars. People would laugh at me when I would talk about those nice things. Deep down, I never wanted to match the normal set standards of life; I wanted to exceed them.

Most often, I would see quotes that resonated with me. The first is, "Someone once told me to not bite off more than I can chew; I told them I'd rather choke on greatness than nibble on mediocrity."

This quote was in my first-ever commercial cleaning contract. I was cleaning by myself, beating myself up, thinking, Did I make a mistake starting this company? That quote hit me hard. I immediately started looking at my business differently. How could I push it to its maximum? How could I succeed? I deserved a seat at the table. If I cannot get a seat at the table, fine. I will build my own dang table! Shifting your mindset from "I cannot do that" to "I can do that" will remove the doubts you thought you had.

A teacher in the fifth grade, I think her name was Mrs. Bender; told us to take "I can't" out of our vocabulary. I subconsciously started doing this even when I was young. I am sure I did not understand it then, but that mind shift is a game changer you will hear from people in all walks of life. It is one of the most powerful tools.

When you believe you deserve it, your whole mindset changes. My mindset changed years ago.

Anything I purchase now, I think to myself, How much money will this make me? How much of my money will this tie up, and for how long?

Some people say, "Fake it till you make it." I can agree with this statement somewhat. You do not have to be perfect in every aspect of business. You need to be consistent and speak confidently in it. Order the top-tier appetizer, sit in First Class, hire the deluxe car ride-share app, and push the luxury button. When you get a taste of what that feels like, it forces you not to accept the bare minimum.

Never associate yourself with these words: Standard, typical, and basic. This is a big motivator for me. I do everything in my power to think outside the box. I seek exclusivity whenever I seek new opportunities; a wealthy mindset is just that. I don't want something everyone else can have. I want something earned. Something unique, something that takes time.

Most people will not bat an eye at the newest smartwatch, but when someone sees Patel Phillippe, they are in awe. Why is that? It's not a timepiece that you see every day. The same rules apply to success. Do you want to be known as a value company associated with cheap? Or do you want to be the quality company that people are willing to pay extra because you go the extra mile to ensure their service?

How do we manifest these options in everyday life?

Manifesting for me started in childhood. I wanted and dreamed of a big, beautiful home. I would see one and burning in the back of my head was the thought: "I deserve that type of home. I will live in in a home like that someday."

Step one is being kind to yourself. Why do you think

many self-made millionaires exist? They normally come from humble beginnings and had no choice but to work extremely hard. They did not ever want to end up back where they started.

There is more than enough room on top for everyone. The question is, how badly do you want it?

It starts with believing in yourself: You deserve it. You are worthy of it. Say it to yourself every morning: "I am worthy." Your mindset will start to shift, small shifts, but shift all the same. Progress, not perfection.

How do you put yourself in a room of people you want to be like? I spoke into existence my dream company, car, and salary. Turn off the phone and pay attention to all the successful people around you. Watch them, study them, and manifest yourself as them. Make up a chart of the things you want. Start small; small milestones are still milestones. Put your name in the middle, then put a few things you want on the farthest end of the paper. Then, draw a line to your name from each of those things. It should make a cross or a star. You are the star in your life.

Then, start following the lineup to the things you would like to obtain. In between your name and your goals, write down small things you can do to obtain these. Please do it for all your goals. These are the building blocks. You should look at these goals multiple times a week.

Place that chart where it will be in your face. In front of your coffee maker, on your fridge, on your mirror—wherever you will see it actively. This is another shift in the right direction. You have heard the term "out of sight, out of mind." The same applies here.

Why do you think you have multiple acquaintances yet only one best friend? You prioritize the best friend. You snap with them daily, talk to them, vacation with them, and always see them. The same rules apply to manifesting. When you consistently seek ways to achieve your goals, they are never on the back burner. Why are the power burners on the front side of the stove? Ease of access and 90 percent of people use that specific burner.

Hopefully, you are starting to see everything in your life is also made up this way. Why is fast food so successful? Ease of access. When I worked at Wendy's, the time to get a customer from the speaker at the drive-through to driving away was sixty seconds. Wendy's has times built into their business. Why? They need to get more transactions, which is how they can charge so little. They have to keep that line free and clear and move people quickly.

If you ever catch an employee hanging out the drive-through window to hit the concrete, this is so they can reset the timer. Normally, the person at the speaker is taking entirely too long. Or the person at the window was taking their time to roll off the timer sensor under the pavement. Again, the same rules apply. Ease of access. How many times have you driven through a drive-through, and that thought never crossed your mind? Now it will.

Paying attention to these small shifts will make your dreams come true faster and keep you consistent in keeping those goals.

Your next manifestation: Dress to impress. Dress for the job you want, not the one you are trying to get. Buy a nice business outfit and watch how people treat you differently. Service will be sub-par when you show up to a restaurant in a hoodie or sweats. Show up dressed like you own the place and watch how the staff treat you. They know you expect the best.

Start demanding what you want from the universe. See how it changes for you. Work until you no longer have to introduce yourself.

When I started my business, I had to tell everyone I was the owner. I was insecure about my position. Now, nine times out of ten, people already know who I am before I enter the room. They know who I am before I sit at the table or when I approach them at a networking or charity event.

When you enter any room, regardless of how you feel, get off your phone. Hold your head up high, scan the room, look back and forth, find who you are looking for, and make eye contact with everyone you pass. That is confidence; those people in that room will remember you made eye contact with them and will come over to introduce themselves to you. Why? You had confidence and that was felt. You shifted the energy in that room.

Do you remember being the light in the darkness? This also applies here. You should not ever feel uncomfortable walking into a room; they should feel uncomfortable that they are not speaking with you.

When I was younger, I was shy; I never liked to approach people. I built my first team of individuals with stronger qualities in the area I lacked. A sales associate who used to work for me could converse with anyone; it was one of her best traits. I have social anxiety but many of my closest colleagues and friends would have no clue. I have been described as the life of the party; people gravitate toward me and my energy is contagious.

I had to overcome what people were thinking of me. I used to walk into those rooms and think, do they like me? Now I walk into those same rooms and wonder, Do I like them?

The quicker you learn this, the better off you will be. They were not ever talking about you. They were not even thinking about you, and guess what? Who cares? You have an empire to build, not people to impress.

I urge you to go to a restaurant and get a table for yourself. Sit with yourself and watch the people around you. Read their body language. What are they talking about? Is this a business lunch or casual? Picking up on energy, body language, and social cues will be great tools when discussing business. You will know when to drop it also when to interject, and when to exit the conversation. After all, your time is precious; you have zero time to waste on petty conversations.

Your tribe should consist of like-minded people who want to grow and build. Find the smartest person in that room and listen to them. Find mentors and take in all of their knowledge. They have failed along the way and will want the next person in line not to fail.

Manifesting the life you want is hard. It is not a quick game either; this is the long game. My friends were clubbing in their early twenties. I was building a brand, a company. One that will change the world. One of the big hitters. One of the greatest. Even though I was doubted along the way, I never gave up. When I see them out, they say, "I never see you at the bar anymore."

My reply is, "Strange, I never see you at the bank. Ha ha"

*Chapter Seventeen*

# The Right Team

We should face it: Rome was not built in a day; most companies, even the fastest-growing ones, are not either. Amazon started in a garage, and my first business also started in my garage. For years, I was the only employee. The number of part-time people that have come and gone is now a distant memory.

In most journeys to success, there will come a time when you are at a hard crossroad: Do I keep pushing, or do I stay content?

When content comes to mind, run as fast as possible. That word is the biggest motivation killer. I took that word out of my vocabulary a long time ago. There is nothing wrong with being a one-person operation. It depends on the depths you are willing to go. I was doing well for only being in a business for a few years. Doubling my salary was great. However, was it only about the money?

I remember coming to this crossroad thinking: I am paying my bills, my business is thriving, I have normalcy back, I work Monday through Friday most days, and I am not working all day or night long. I look forward to the weekend, and I live for the weekend.

The answer is no. I did not start this business so I could make tons of money. I started this business so I could have my life back. I could have my time back. Those sacrifices I made initially, wishing I could have spent more time with my sister, weigh so heavily now.

Those shoes that are $120, are they worth the twelve hours you had to put in if you were making $10 an hour? So one pair of shoes costs you an entire day of your life. It's all about the mindset.

I wanted my time back, but then I thought: What happens when I get older and cannot work as much and as hard? Who picks up my shift when I am unable to? Who picks it up when I am sick? I would have to work harder the next day or lose an entire day of not making anything.

That was not personally going to work for me. It is time to hit that drawing board again. I had to scale the business larger to pay someone to help me cover my shift more efficiently. If I paid someone a portion of that, I could buy back more time throughout the week and have zero to worry about on the weekend.

You eventually will learn hiring friends and family is not the best idea. Sometimes, it works, but very seldom is that the case.

I started trying to find the right fit for this position. Qualities had to be perfect: they had to mirror my exact moves. They had to be me when I was not looking. One thing they don't tell you is that this will be tough to find, though not impossible. Finding the person who will fit this spot takes a lot of errors and mistakes. I had many employees come and go, and most of the time, I would get stuck cleaning all by myself. When people do not own something, it is typically hard to get them to care. That is just the name of the game.

I tell my employees, "I will not expect you to bleed out for this job. However, best believe I hired you for a position and I expect that position to be done correctly. I don't have the time to micro-manage."

Typically, giving employees their own space to make errors and learn will help you get better results. That said, do not make the same mistake I made for several years. There needs to be expectations and accountability: You must train them, and I mean train them. They need a full breakdown of their job expectations, and they need the full breakdown of what happens when these expectations do not get handled. Otherwise, they are going to be winging it.

This step commonly gets overlooked when you have many things coming at you in every direction. Hear me out. This step should never be overlooked. That can cause you astronomical problems.

Clear and concise guidelines will keep the ship heading in the right direction. You want to be able to trust your employees are doing the right thing when you cannot watch. Find that person who is coachable. You can hire some of the most experienced people and pay a pretty penny for them. However, that does not ensure your success, and sometimes those people form bad habits.

I always said I am willing to hire anyone. Most of the time, stay-at-home parents are the best people to train. They have kids all day long, all night long, all weekend long. For that reason, they have to be resilient; they have to be quick; they have a sense of urgency; they have to be efficient. As most of us know, kids do not wait for anyone. Their adaptability is unmatched. Most people typically do not do well with change, but they encourage change. I also encourage change. It keeps things interesting it also keeps people engaged.

It took me years to find people that I could rely on. I tell my employees, "It's okay if you don't like me if I have earned your respect."

I think a common misconception is that you hire someone, and they automatically follow suit and do their jobs. Not even close. As the leader of the company. Your employees need to follow you. How do you get them to do that? You must, and I say must, earn their respect. Treat them great, train them well, and make them want to improve themselves. Again, this will take a lot of sacrifice on your part. If their kids are sick, you step in and take over the rest of their shift. Let them be with their kids when needed. Do not, and I repeat, do not guilt them into staying. Would you want to get your kids if the roles were reversed? You would, so why expect anything different from them? Do they look tired at work? Ask them if they are okay. If they need time, ask if they want to take the afternoon off. Everyone you meet is struggling with something.

When I was little, I wanted someone to see me and tell me it was all right. Maybe that is what they need. Again, in a world where you can be anything, be kind. These small little acts of kindness breed respect. You are never too big not to understand what a human needs. Your success is paramount to your employees. If they believe in you and themselves, they will believe in changing this world. Your clients will see this in your vision, how you gave your employees the same opportunity that your clients gave you. It builds a strong foundation for your company.

Most leadership books will tell you to lead by example, and your people will follow suit. I had an employee who had wildly followed me into the depths of hell, and we both came out stronger on the other side. You need one to follow you, and it will slowly grow from there.

People want to be heard, see change, and be respected. I struggle to tell you how often I have had to cancel vacations or dinner plans because my employees needed me. The investment will outweigh the sacrifice twofold.

Jump in those pits now and again with your people. Invest in your people. Take time to get to know them. We have a sheet every new employee fills out when they start. It's like a fun facts sheet. Super simple questions like, what's your favorite color, what's your favorite food? These sheets come in handy when you see someone going up over and beyond; how do you reward them? Yes, money is a good factor, but that is not the simple answer anymore. People nowadays want flexibility. They do not care about all the hours and money. They want to have a strong work-home life balance coupled with flexibility. When you see them excelling, you get them a thoughtful gift that requires effort. The results are amazing.

Learn about every one of your employees; they will battle for you repeatedly. Employees who feel valued and appreciated will always put their best efforts forward. They become your brand ambassadors. They say the greatest things about the company to strangers. Not only do they want other people to work there, but they want people to see the foundation of this company is solid, and as a client, it will be worth the future investments when they use your services. It becomes contagious and before you know it, you have zero turnover in an industry that normally has a short employee shelf life. Then you have a team backing you, all pushing us to be better versions of ourselves!

You must structure your company and employees to do the right thing when no one is looking. Hold quarterly meetings to check in with your team. Give them anonymous surveys to fill out. See if there is something they would like to see changed or improved within your company. Remember, your team should consist of people with strengths in the departments you lack. You will not know everything you have to continue learning.

Make a space where your employees can be heard with no backlash. They will be some of your most important assets; ensure you are doing right by them. This space can let you get ahead of any issues that may arise. You want them to come forward when something bothers them. The last thing anyone wants is a top employee randomly quitting and never hearing from them again. When this happens, you should know you failed that employee. If you have no idea why they quit, you should quickly understand why and how that happened. That employee felt unheard and felt it didn't matter what they said, and they exited their job, lit that bridge on fire, and never looked back. You should be able to speak to them like anyone else, and they should be comfortable coming forward.

You wonder, but what if I train them so well and they leave? GOOD! They have the right to leave. However, if you train and treat them well, they will not want to leave. The workforce nowadays could not care less about money; they are about working to live, not living to work like our previous generations. We have employees leave, and most of the time, they come back. Why? They see that we do care about the people on our team. They are not numbers.

I admit when employees label our clients "customers," I correct them. Customers are for fast food; clients are the people we do business with. We take the opportunity to get to know our clients and our employees. Our clients are not just numbers. They are people. This quality approach ensures value and the continued success of our brand. They used us once three years ago, but they remembered how kind and generous we were, so they called us again.

This should be the core of your culture. Why do we do the right things? We do this because it is the right thing to do.

# Chapter Eighteen

# Row or Drill

Getting a team in place is only half the battle; keeping them in place is a completely different ball game. People have asked me what the hardest part of my job is. It is not the hours, most certainly not the tasks or the multiple divisions. The hardest part of my job is managing people.

Think about this: You have a team of twenty. Twenty personalities, twenty mindsets, twenty different mood swings, twenty mind-thought processes, twenty different pains, and twenty different goals. One conversation might be super helpful with one employee, but that same conversation could be useless with another. When I told you to sit alone at a restaurant and observe people, this is where that comes into play.

These tools will come in handy. They will be a part of your everyday life, both personal and business. Your approach must be Switzerland, just neutral. You will always have a different experience than the person sitting across from you. Listen intently before you respond. The goal is not to win, the goal is to understand. When that person feels heard and safe, the walls come tumbling down. They will give you all the answers you need.

Most of the time it has nothing to do with you or business. Normally it is underlying issues or personal issues that have unfortunately rolled over into their workday. This is okay, it happens. Let them know that it is okay. We are all human and we all make mistakes. Now this should not happen every day or week, but it does happen.

You have to learn not to take things personally and how to read people. You have to learn how to guide them back onto the ship. The ship must keep pushing forward. We may hit a bump or seven, but the ship must keep going forward.

When you don't hit these problems head on, this is where resentment builds. Making no decision will always be the wrong decision. Even if they make the wrong decision, at least they made one. We can explain to them why that would be the wrong decision, and we can move forward with clarity.

When no decisions are made, the problems heighten. They gain momentum. They spread. Like a dam a beaver builds, this slows the flow and creates a barrier between you and the employees. The only way through that dam after its built is destruction, and it will be a mess when tearing it down to get the ship flowing again.

If you want this business to operate like a fine oiled machine, this cannot keep happening. Resentment builds, feelings are left unsaid, and a cancer of toxicity spreads. Cancer starts from the inside out. So many times, it is caught too late and the damage is done. Never allow it to spread. Keep a tight hand on it. This cancer will divide the ship, pushing employees to draw a line on the deck. This could be with or without management. The longer it continues the more dangerous it becomes.

The first step is stopping the mess in its tracks. Correct issues quickly and abruptly. Go back to the basics of your core values. How far away are you from the values? How quickly can you get them back? The ship is headed for the rocks; we must tip it on its side so we can flow over them with as little damage as possible.

As management, you should take the blame if you were

the problem. Humanize yourself. Start by apologizing for failing them. Sometimes we will not see it coming and that is the truth. Let them voice their frustrations. This should never get to an elevated level, since you have earned their respect. Keep calm and stay neutral. If their tone gets a bit too amplified, slowly and calmly ask them if they need a moment to gather themselves. Again, humanizing yourself. The last thing you want is a screaming match.

When they get to the end of their sentence, replay it back for them and tell them you are just trying to understand. Acknowledge their feelings. Let them know this is a safe space. Understand they are human too. I like to use the line, "I see you and I hear you." This normally lowers frustration on their part.

A lot of this drama will consist of something that was taken out of context, resulting in their with their emotions running the show. The storyline will be so far twisted sometimes. Offer them clarity if you are wrong and apologize. Acknowledge that a mistake has been made, and that you will do better moving forward. Make sure to let them unpack all the baggage and issues. You need to figure out what went wrong.

A common issue is that the tasks you decided to delegate were not delegated to the front runners, and now everyone is confused about what is expected. You also must be very sure when you delegate that tasks are being delegated in the manner how you said they should be. Find the kink in the chain; trust me, there is one. Also get everyone's side. See who is the one not making decisions or who is being a little too soft with relaying the issue.

This can be difficult in our current times. People feel being direct is being mean. That is not the case. Just because they do not like the answer does not mean you are attacking them.

After that situation is back under control, does the ship still seem off? Make sure everyone is helping row that ship, and that they aren't drilling holes in the bottom of it.

Time and time again you will run into an employee that is so good at their job, everyone loves them—clients and managers. Most of the time, almost all your team members do not like them. I do not care how good someone is at their job. If they are drilling holes and they are the cancer in the company, cut ties immediately. Nothing will kill a great employee quicker than watching a business tolerating a terrible one. Trim that fat quickly.

I learned this lesson the hard way. I have learned it several times over the years. This is why it is so important to make decisions and make them quickly and correctly. We all have seen this employee, the one where you are like, How did you even get hired here in the first place? They put on a show, but their attitude can be so foul behind closed doors. The bosses love them, and they are terrible to other employees. They secretly sabotage the company but lie to the owner's faces. They only care for themselves.

Remember, when someone shows you exactly who they are you should believe them. They could be your biggest performer, your biggest money maker. If they are toxic, they are toxic. Cut the cord. Do not tolerate it. This is why the ship is divided and heading for the rocks, you already knew the answer you now must make the decision.

You will lose people along the way. If they cannot align with the culture, they cannot level up with the company. You cannot hold back your company for one employee. Again, I do not care how good of a worker they are. They are cancer that will keep coming back and eating your business. Fuck cancer. That should always be the motto. You must have everyone rowing to keep the ship afloat and keep the ship navigating in the right direction at all times. That kind of cancer can take a company out of business for good. Get back on the path and keep moving forward. Your crew will respect you so much more if you make the hard decisions quickly.

You must lead by example in these situations. You must set a standard with hard boundaries. You will be tempted to bend the rules to allow certain behaviors. There is a reason those policies have been put in place. You will be tested. You will have to fire your best or favorite employee. You cannot bend the rules. The boundaries are to be followed. You cannot show favoritism to employees. Every single employee and manager should be held to the same standard. These should not be up for discussion.

As the old saying goes, "Do not mix business with pleasure." It cannot be truer than in this context. As an owner, you had a standard to set. You should not be hanging out with employees after hours for fun. It sets a weird tone for other employees. Trust me, do not put yourself in these situations. The lines always get crossed or blurred. Then a correction must be made. Things get weird, and ill feelings get harbored.

If you are in management, the same rules apply. Being friends with your employees very seldom works out. It always ends badly. Keep your boundaries in check. If you are invited to something that might put you in a weird light, kindly decline and explain why it would not be a good position for either one of you to be in. Professionalism should always be locked in place. It is there for a reason.

This brings up another topic: Your coworkers or managers are not your friends. They come to work for the same reason you do. You are here to get paid for the work you do. We see this time and time again. The more of your personal life you discuss at work, the more it is going to be used against you. When push comes to shove, and it comes down to their job or yours, they will inevitably throw you under the bus to save their job.

I will tell everyone who works with me: "Your words will always be used against you." So do not put yourself in those types of situations. You are there to work, so why complicate things. Life is hard enough as it is. Stop making it harder.

Go to work, do your job, go home.

One of my favorite lines I used when I was a manager was, "I have plenty of friends. I am not here to make friends; I am here to make money." That is a good phrase to keep in the back of your mind. Sure, it is always a bonus when you have great coworker that make you enjoy being at work. That is why your culture is so important. Keep the company a great place to work and you will have no problems with staffing or succeeding.

Good things take time. Keep grinding and building, make hard decisions fast. Show up, do your best, your team and dreams will follow.

# Chapter Nineteen

# Through the Glass House

Why do we throw stones when every one of us lives in a glass house? I think throwing stones and casting judgment is easy. Depth is hard. If you want to succeed, get ready for a deep dive. I mean the deepest dive you will ever take. The only way to succeed is to grow. Grow wiser. Keep learning.

If I lined up the times I have doubted myself, the length of that line would be astounding. I think that our own self-doubt will break us down quicker than anyone ever could. You can let your circumstances define you or let them thrive you.

Pick your hard: working out is hard, getting up early is hard, working a lot is hard. Anything in life that is hard, is worth having. Everyone gets to see the results of success not what drove them. They do not get to see what put them there, or what built them.

What a perfect world it could be if we could see and hear what people are thinking. I used to hide my experiences, fear of judgment, fear of my own shame, fear of pity. I would not change my story, because if I did, I would not be trying to write this book. If one person can read this and it helps them, I consider this book a success. It does not have to be a best seller or make the most money.

I was put on this earth to do epic shit; I was put here to help people. If you are transparent, you will be heading toward success. I believe transparency is beneficial in business. I will be the first to show anyone what they want or need to see. A lot of people will doubt this step. I also doubted this step. You think opening your business makes you vulnerable, it does not. If you are open-minded and explain to people why things are the way they are, they too can grow. They get a deeper understanding of life and business if we share why we take all the risks, and why we do at times reap the rewards.

Break down every aspect of your business if your employee asks. Allow them to ask questions in a safe, healthy environment.

I truly think people are so unaware of the cost associated with just operating a legitimate business. Taxes alone are a big expense for small businesses. I tell my employees all the time that Plan B does not exist for me. This is the only plan I have. I do not have a safety net anymore. It is all a risk and hopefully a reward.

My employees can walk away tomorrow and go find another job. Have you ever given the business owner a second thought? I urge you to humanize yourself. Think about if the roles were reversed. Most business owners have tons of debt they are forced to carry. When you allow your employees to see these debts, these responsibilities, this risk, they will see you as human. Not as a bank account. I have had numerous conversations about how I am not able to draw a check from my company. Why? You must pay your employees first. As an owner you will be on the back burner most of the time.

You must be smart about enjoying the fruits of your labor. Most businesses fail due to cash flow. Some owners will bleed the businesses dry. This is not the way to operate. Do you want a short-lived success? Or do you want a lifetime of success?

Transparency plays such a vital role in building and maintaining success. Discipline in business is hard. I think we all are guilty of saying "I've earned it" or "I've put in the work; I deserve to be rewarded" or "I deserve a break." I too have fallen into this thought process, but the work is never done when you own a business. It requires consistent monitoring and consistent growth.

Let your employees in. Let them see the good, the bad, and the ugly. Now I am not saying everyone deserves an explanation of why things operate the way they do. You don't have to give everyone an answer. Consider each scenario and ask yourself, "Is this person able to comprehend the dept of this conversation?" If the answer is no, move on. Let them have their wrong ideas and be wrong. Who cares. You have an empire to grow. Bees will never explain to flies why honey is better than poop. Invest in those who invest in you.

When your employees can see how to reap better rewards from their job well done, they subconsciously will start to gravitate toward making the business better. Everyone gets to win. When business is booming, everyone reaps the ultimate benefits. You will see great results in this. Grow a business where people are included in decisions, where their voice matters, that their opinions matter, and it will make positive change. Everyone wants to feel valued.

New employees see me now and they assume I was handed this life with my privilege. I like to let them assume. When they look past the shell of success, they see I was just another little hillbilly kid with a dream. I am now living the life I wanted.

You become a great leader when you help everyone who works for you reach their own goals. You teach them for free. You train them for free. We all are on a journey, and there is more than enough room on top.

When I was younger, it was safer to hide who I was. Do not let them know you do not have hot water. Do not let them know you barely slept last night, due to all the arguing and the constant state of panic you live in. Do not let them know you are so overly envious of their family time, yearning for their closeness as a family.

I used to bury this part of my life. The truth is if my life had been anything other than what it was, I would not be the man I am today. I am so thankful that even in success I can still relate to the struggles of people.

At my wedding, I wanted everyone at the same table. I will forever till the end of time have this mindset. If you have more than enough, build a bigger table, not a higher wall. Everyone deserves a seat if they are willing to sacrifice for it. Everything in life comes with sacrifice.

I did have to carve out a different path and build my own table. I was different. I was told over and over I could not sit at the table. I built my own. Guess what? Everyone has a seat.

We grow when we are challenged. How boring of a life would it be if we all did the same thing? We would all be sheep. You should challenge the normal. Explain your story. Let them see through the glass house. Let them see the cracks, let them see the levels, let them see the plastic, that had to be molded to keep the house together. Let them see the shattered rooms when you and your business fell apart. Show them the adhesive you used to glue it back together.

These cracks and seams will help your employees understand why you had to work so hard. Why you still to this day bleed out for your company. It is your heart, your own vision, it is your drive, it is your normalcy. They will align themselves to your dream. They will help you get where you want to go. You will, in turn, be helping them obtain their own goals. Get to know them, get to know their glass houses. The leaders in our company lead by this example.

I always say, "Want to start a business? I will show you how."

Starting a business is not easy. It is not luck it is not a brand it is not money. If you are thinking about it, congratulations. Most people won't even take a step to try.

You are ahead of 90 percent of your competition.

Keep transparency at the forefront of your business and you will find success that you never thought was possible. Keeping it in every aspect of life will align you better than any false narrative you could ever make up. People do not resonate with fake and surface, they resonate with deep. Why is this book compelling? It evoking interest, attention, or admiration in a powerfully, irresistible way.

They say you should not throw stones when you live in a glass house. The meaning behind this is that people who have faults should not criticize other people for having faults. We all are guilty of this at times. You should look at the glass houses full of faults and try to understand them. Do not criticize them, try to understand them. Try to learn from them. Have empathy. Have remorse. Have self-reflection. Put yourself in their shoes. Would you have reacted any differently if you were them? Then grow from it. Teach from it.

We should try to do better moving forward. Own our faults. Love those faults. We will use them for the better, to build something we all can be proud of. Time is limited. How will you spend it? I want to spend my time smashing through walls, breaking the glass, and rebuilding the better homes. The warm one, the bent one, the broken one, the rebuilt one. The imperfectly built one.

*Chapter Twenty*

# **Our Scars Are Beautiful**

The scars that form us are just that. They are not so pretty. But what those scars have been built from is beautiful. Sure, everyone dreams of having perfect skin with no scars. I find little to no scars to be boring. If you do not have battle wounds, have you experienced life changing events? Pain is awful but it is how we grow and learn. You touch a hot pan, it burns your hand, typically you will not make that mistake again. The same applies to everyday life and success. My scars are beautiful, both internal and external. Some of the best stories have scars. At least you can try to hear those scars, learn to appreciate those scars when you reach your level of success.

Success has so many different meanings to so many different people. I urge you to ask people you know from all different walks of life what success looks like for them. Success to me means I am comfortable. I don't have to stress over whether I've achieved what I wanted in my life. It is my time being spent doing meaningful work. My time being spent gathering memories I will cherish for the rest of my life.

When you ask all your friends and family about success, study them. What does it mean to you? Is building this business going to align you with those goals? What world will you leave behind for the next generations?

You inevitably will get to a place where you feel the most humbling experience. I felt that experience when I hit a milestone I thought was never obtainable. Our company made $100,000 in sales in one month. Historically speaking, this month was always the slowest time for the company, and we blew the roof right off.

With tear-soaked and exhausted eyes, I could not believe we did it. I could not believe that this little hillbilly boy could, and did achieve this. It was such a beautiful moment for me. One I will cherish for the rest of my life.

Looking at this milestone, making it through the pandemic of COVID19. I wanted to quit. I wanted to sell. We have been approached to sell our company. I would be lying if I said it was not enticing to walk away from it all and still have money left over for another venture. I would have had considerably less stress and pain. Then it hit me: To sell my name to someone I don't know. For what? A quick buck? Remember I always take the path with significantly more resistance. How could I sell my name? My brand? My identity?

Time to dig in my heels in and tear at those scars some more. We then went on to understand the ups and downs of businesses. We changed what needed to be changed. Fixing our own scars.

Then something beautiful happened. I now own one of the most desirable cleaning businesses in Cincinnati. Not only did everyone want a piece of it. We again hit another sales milestone: We hit $100,000 in sales in one month AGAIN. Wow! Twice and almost three times in one year! That year we closed out at our highest on record. We hit $1.1 million in sales.

You see, when things are tough, and you want to give up, please don't. Keep pushing. I promise, you will be so proud of yourself. If I sold out, I would have never been able to figure out what that feels like.

Statistically speaking, most small businesses in my industry are not able to obtain what we did. I was doubted the whole way, I was told it would not work, I was told it was not possible. It is possible, if you change your mindset and stare at those scars. They will be the best reminders of why you started.

If you ever find yourself living in a monumental moment such as this, turn around and look back at all those steps, bumps, and scars that put you here. Thank your team, thank your clients, thank your family, thank your friends. Whether they were good and positive or bad and negative, their words and actions helped you achieve this amazing goal. Congratulations, you are in the top 9 percent of small businesses. Only 9 percent of small businesses reach $1 million or more in sales revenue.

What to do now? You reached a milestone most people will never ever get to reach. Pat yourself on the back. Take a few days and reflect on all the scars. You have earned it. You made it. Through perseverance, you have beat the odds.

I was the little hillbilly boy. I was the one who would not make it. I had seen too much. Too much pain, too much trauma, too much hate, too much to carry. I made it.

Just remember to be kind to yourself. You are doing better than you think. I am the proof. You do not have to be defined by your upbringing or your circumstances. I am the Other American Dream. I could not be here without those awful scars. I love them now. I am proud of them. I love their imperfections. They are like me: messy, jagged, and with different depths. They are resilient.

So, what do you do now that you beat those odds? Now it's time to smash the hell out of those odds. How do we get to another level of growth? Time to fail again, time to learn. Time to shake it up.

Complacency is a motivation killer. You could stay at this level if you chose, however how much more capable are you? Do you want to be ordinary? Or do you want to be extraordinary? How can you improve your current odds? You already beat the other odds; these ones will be much easier. You will not be starting from scratch; you are starting from experience. How do you level up again? You owe it to yourself.

You have come this far. Keep going! I am so proud of you! Time to scale the operations of your business. How do you go from $1.1 million in sales to $3 million? Reflection is crucial, success is not given, it is earned. Keep pushing yourself to new lengths. Remember the average millionaire has seven streams of income.

Here is your next goal. Invest in yourself. Invest in your brand. You will be the definition of success one day! Keep on winning at the game of life!